Tabby's Tangled Art Ultimate Coloring Collection 2

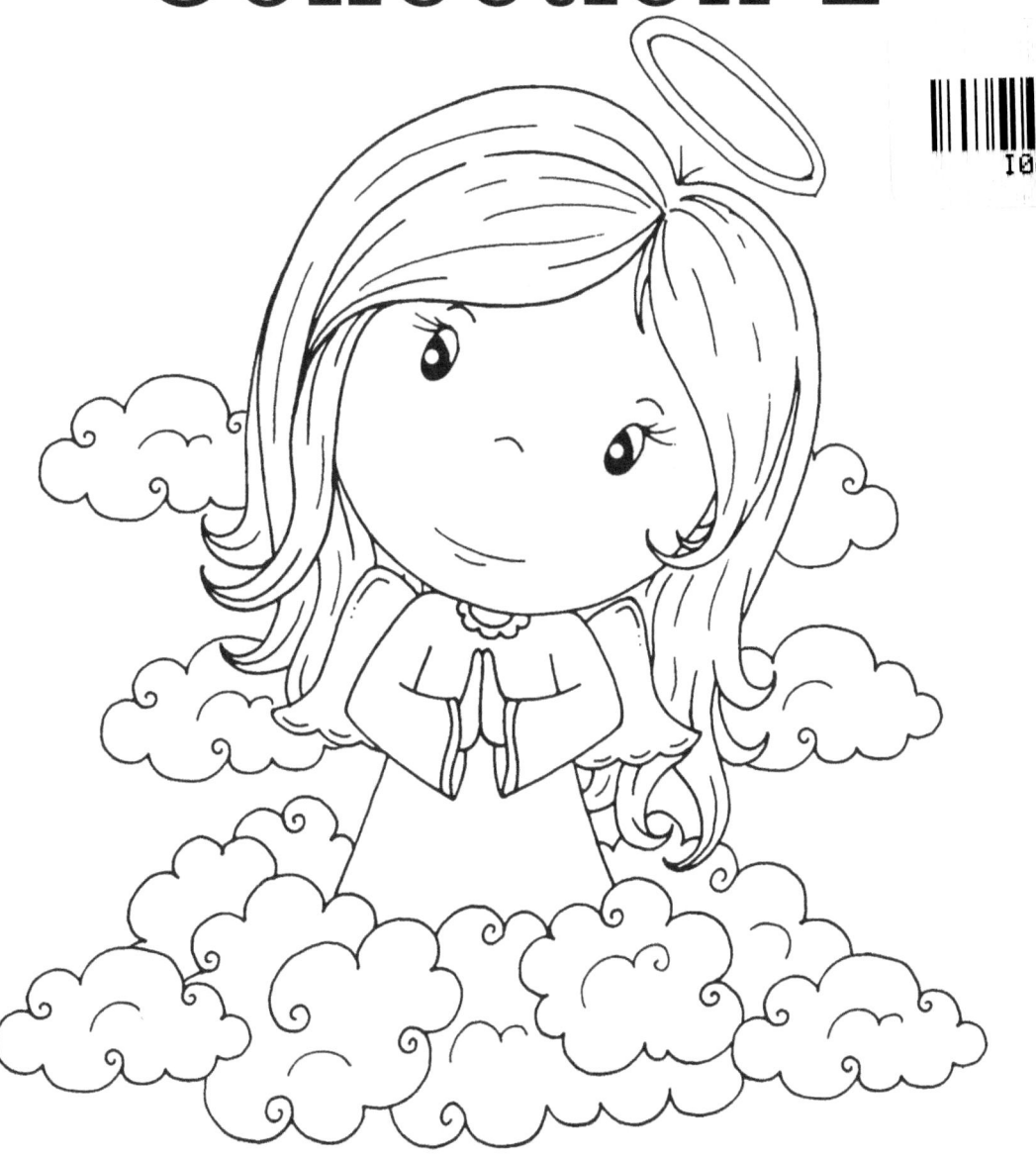

Copyright ©2019 Tabitha L. Barnett

This publication is protected by copyright law. Please respect the law. No part of this publication can be republished, reused, reproduced or stored in a database retrieval system without prior written consent from the artist. The one exceptjion to this is that you may photocpy pages for PERSONAL USE ONLY.

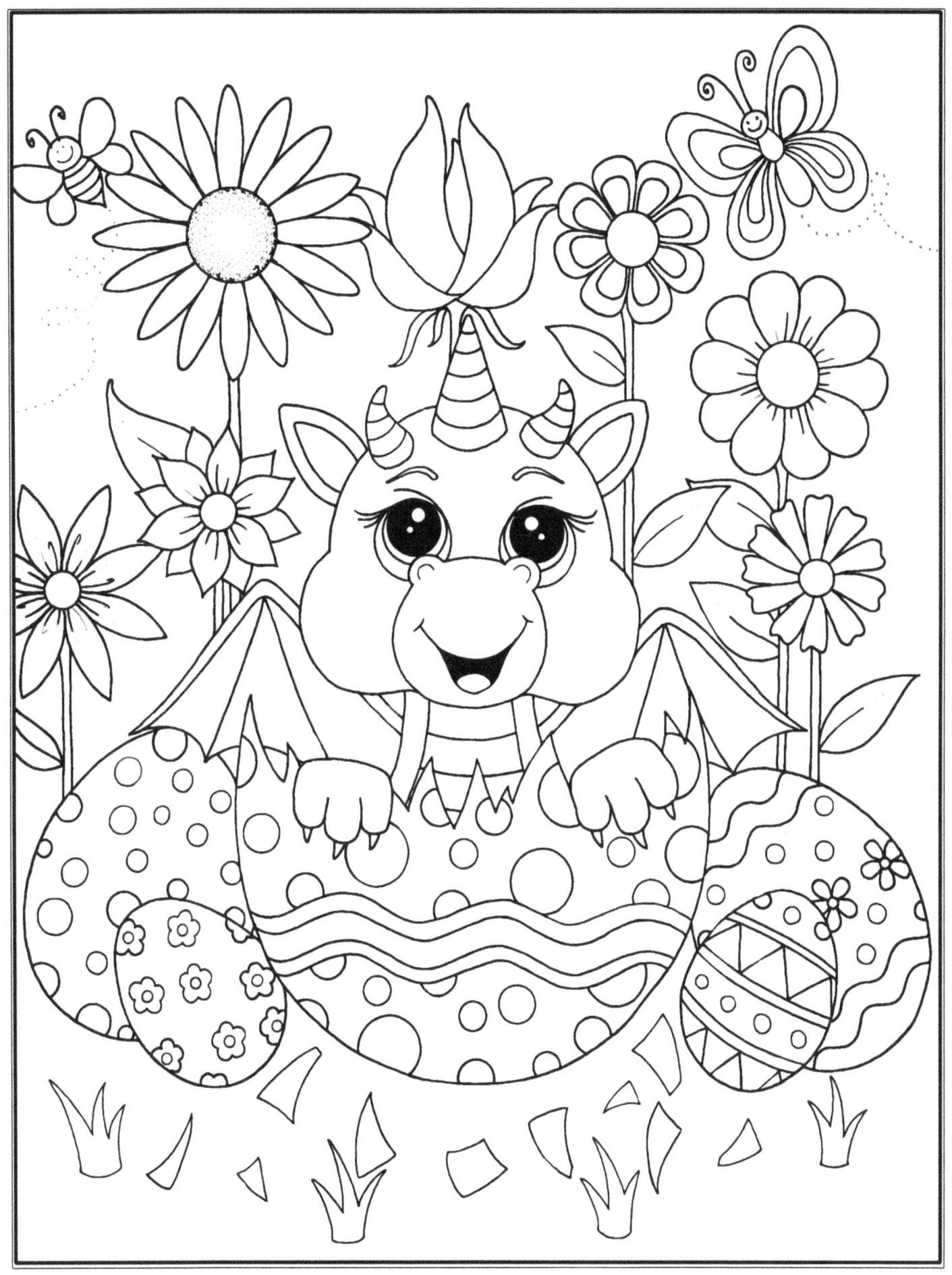

Adorable Easter © 2019 Tabitha Barnett

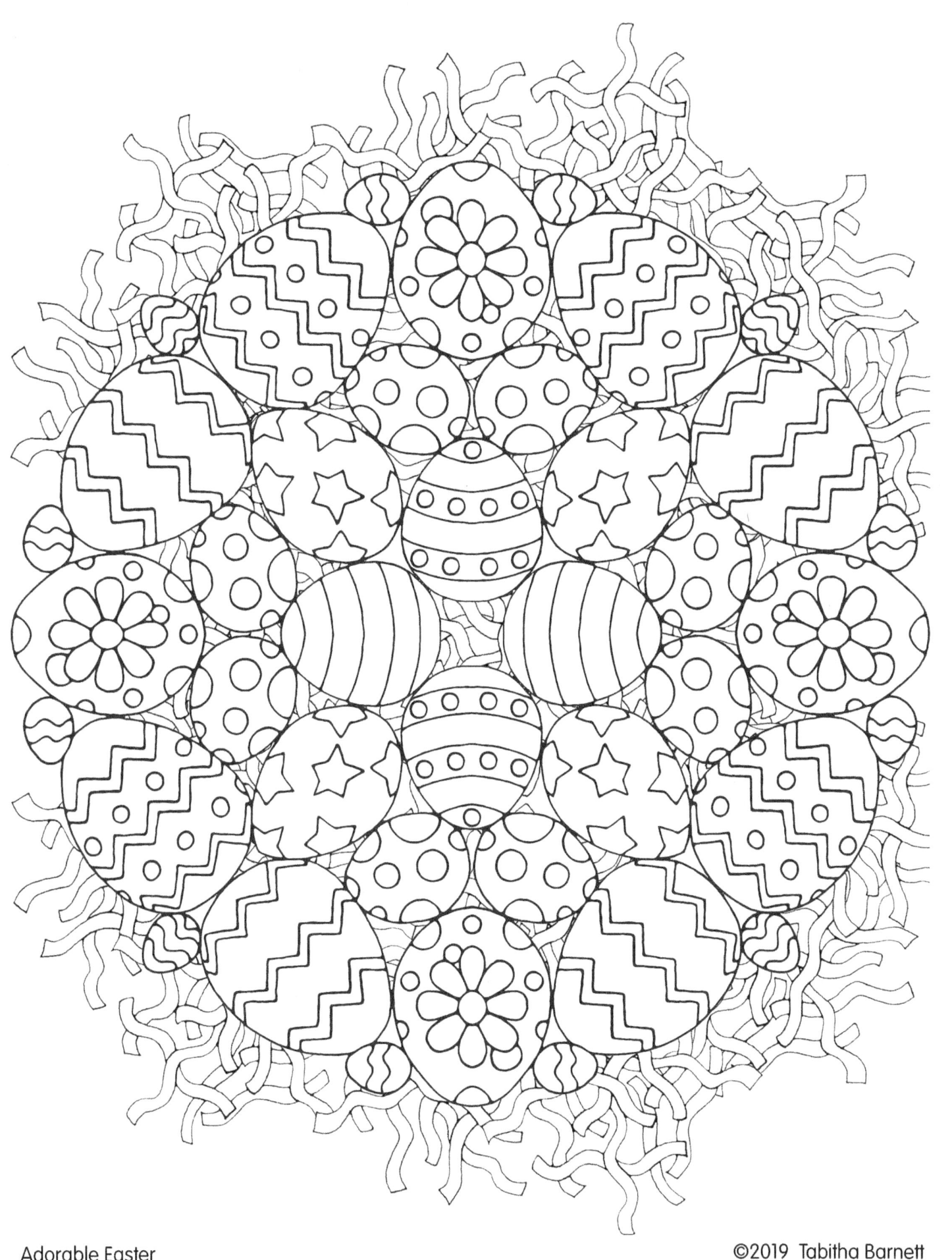

Adorable Easter © 2019 Tabitha Barnett

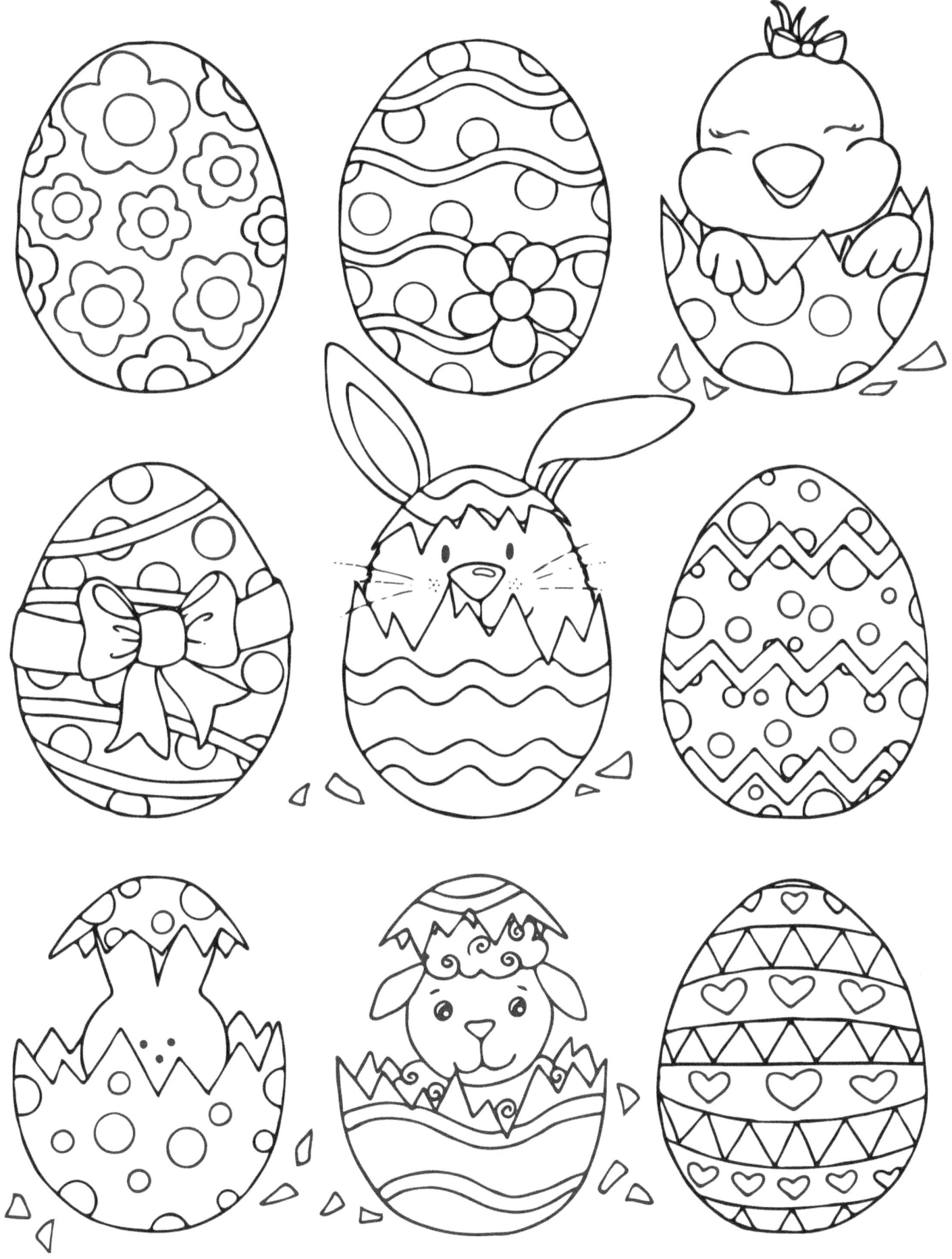

Adorable Easter ©2019 Tabitha Barnett

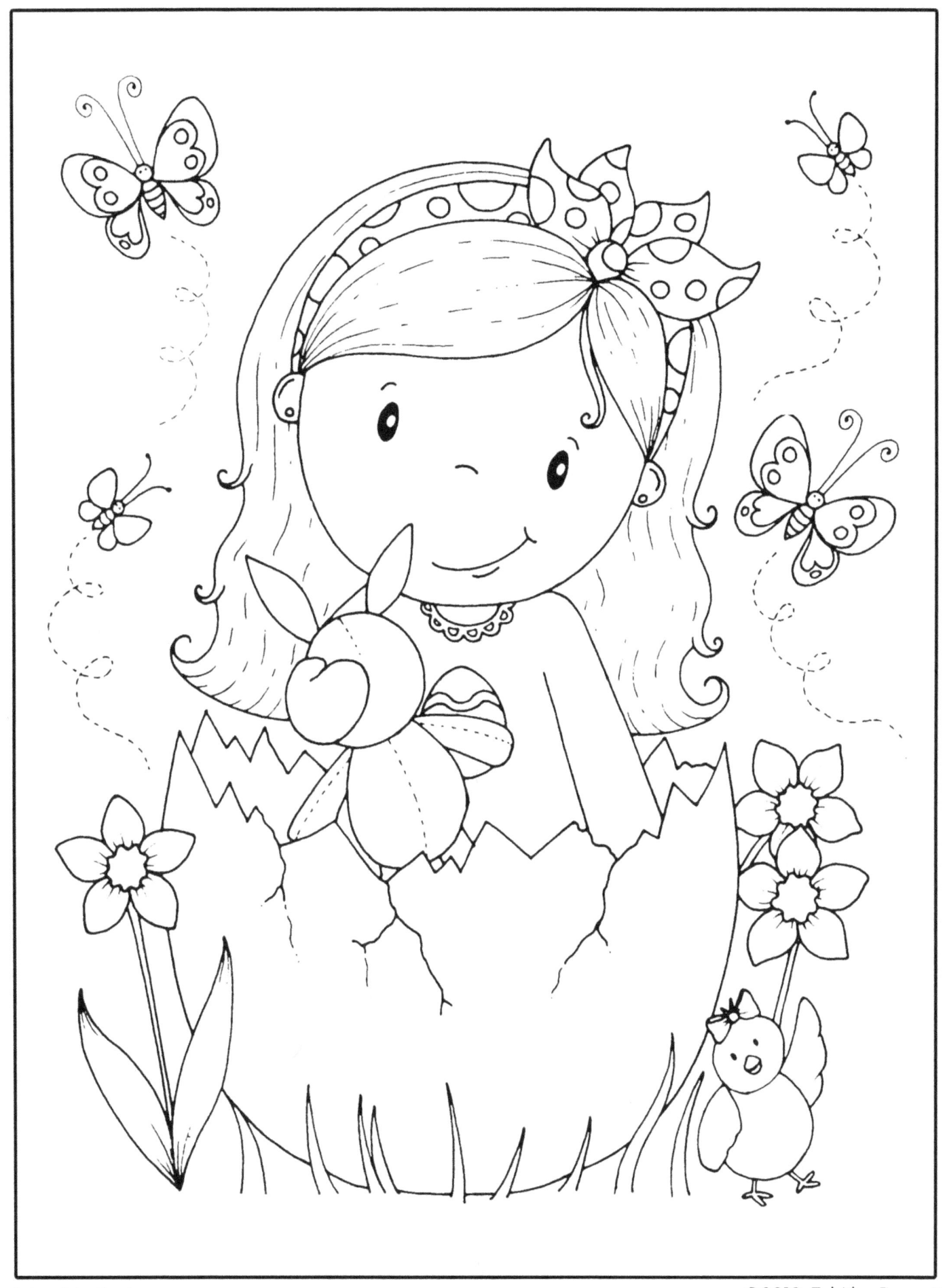

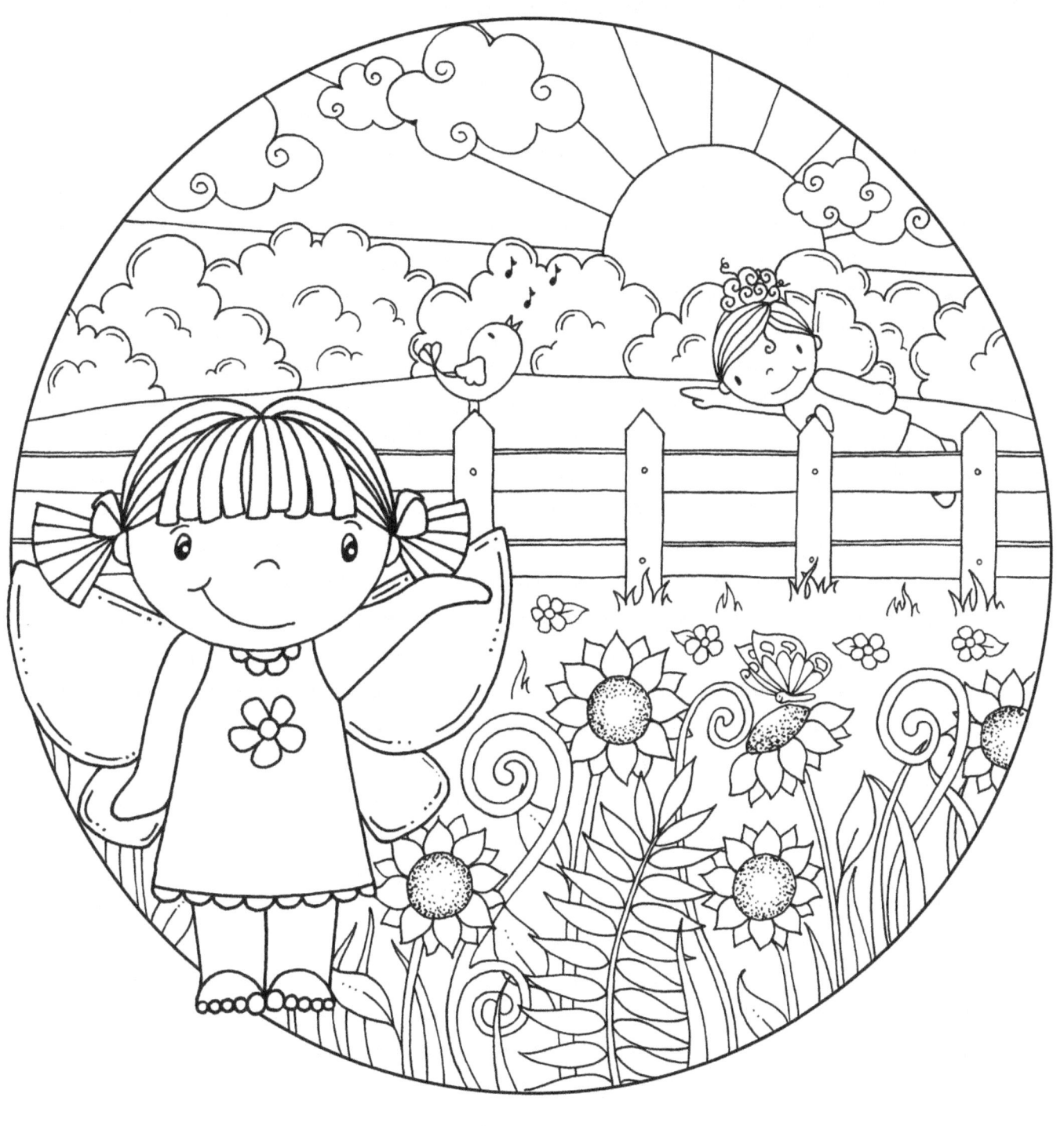

A Fairies Tale

©2019 Tabitha Barnett

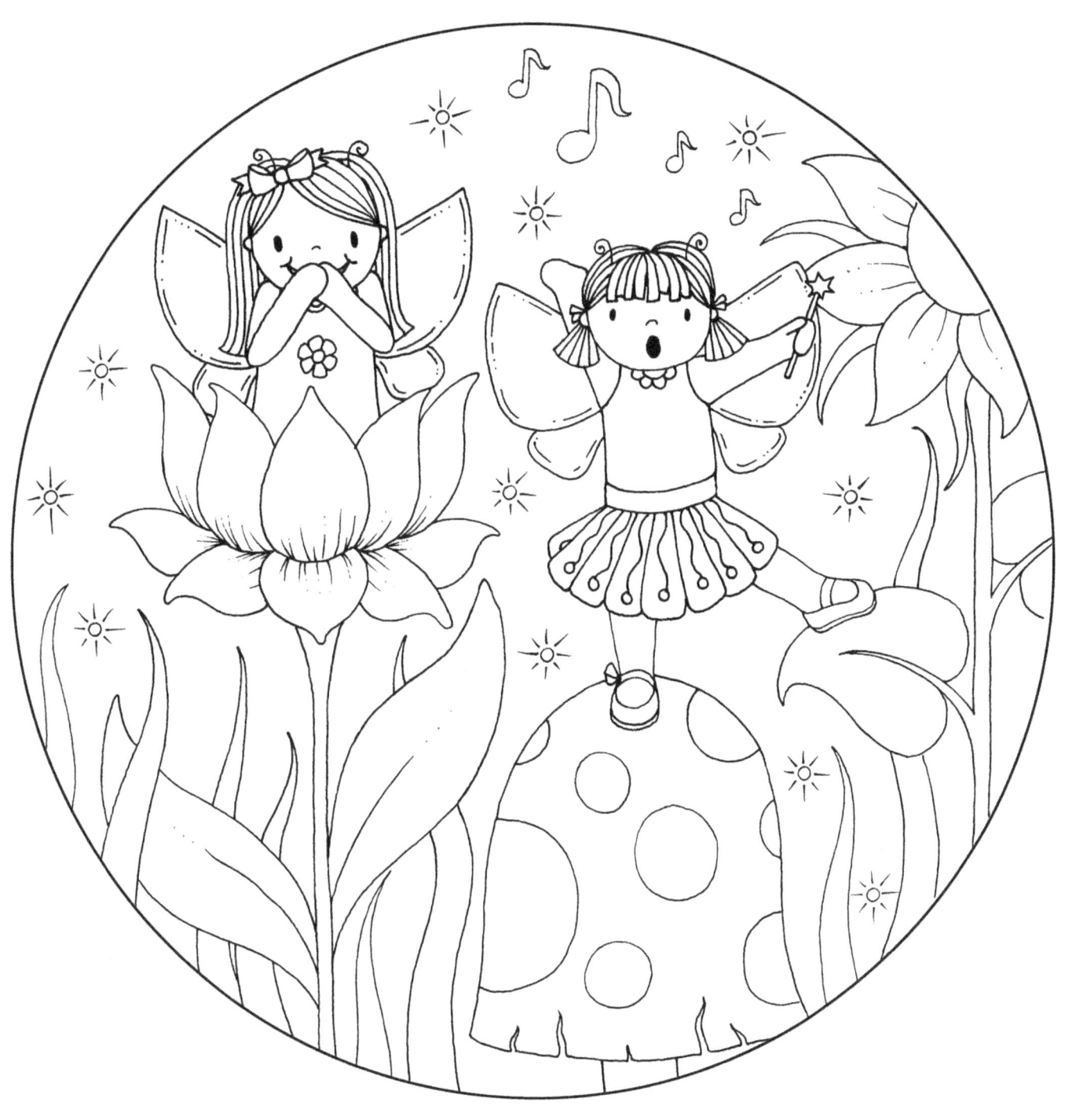

A Fairies Tale ©2019 Tabitha Barnett

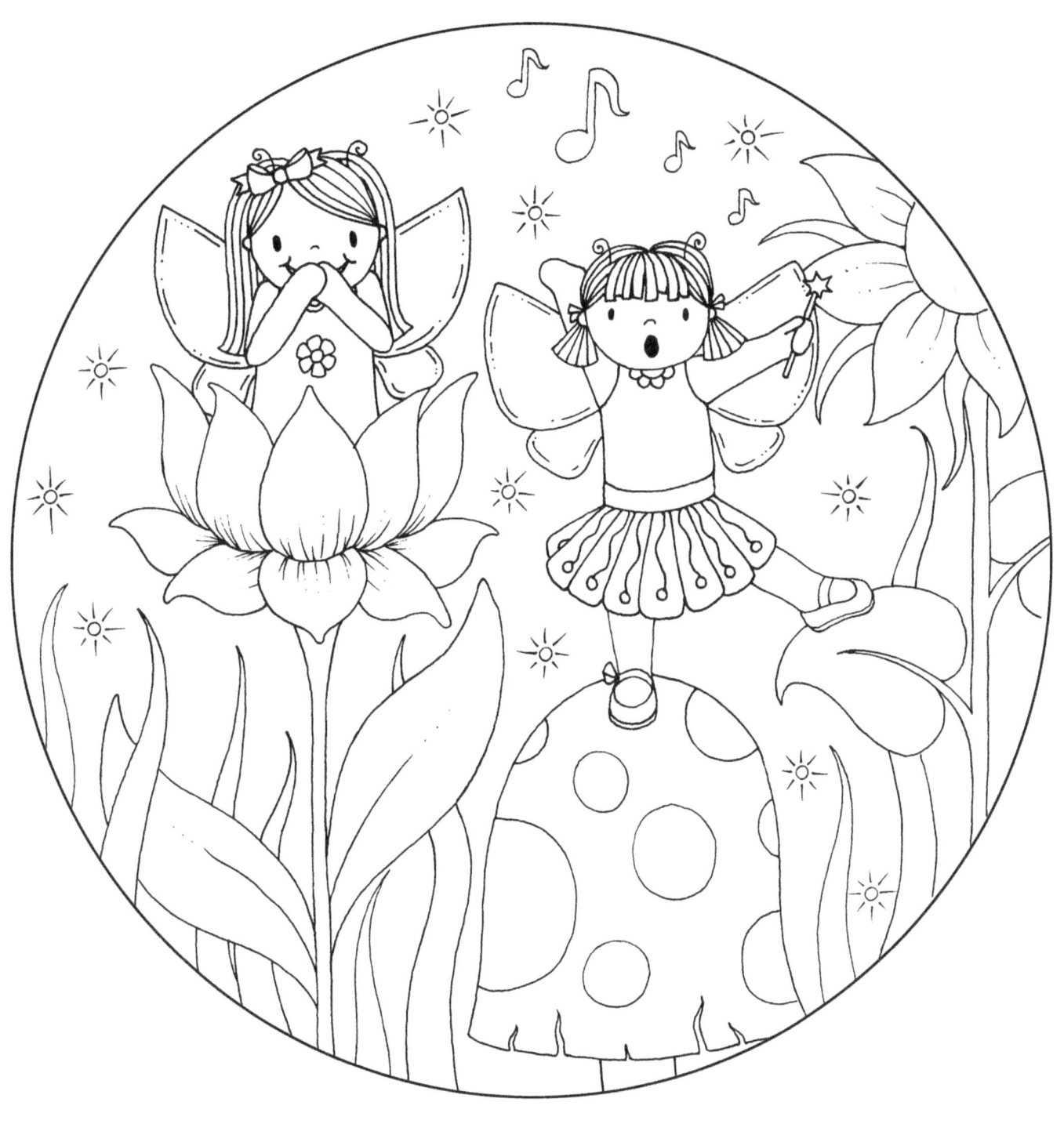

A Fairies Tale

©2019 Tabitha Barnett

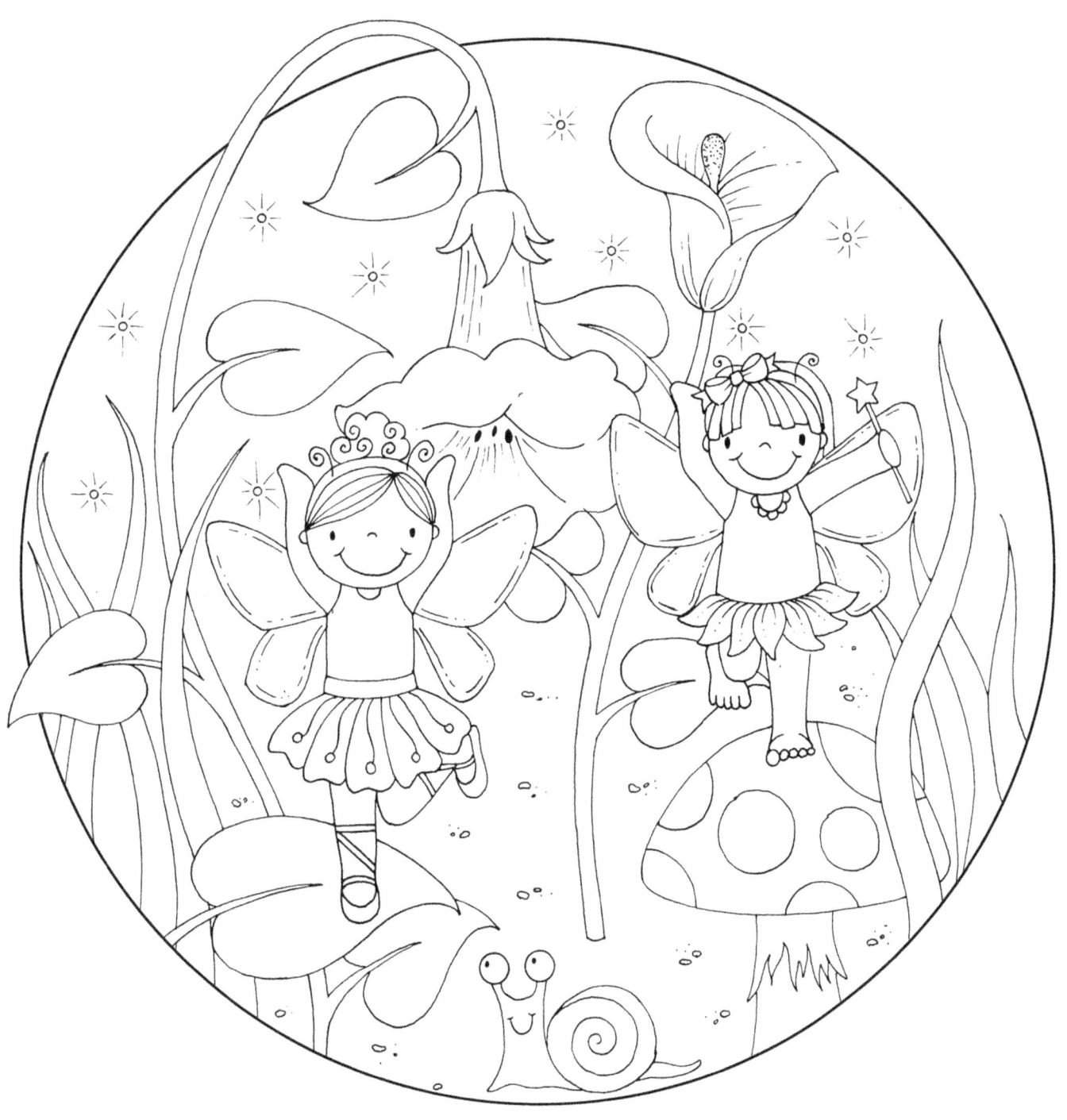

A Fairies Tale

©2019 Tabitha Barnett

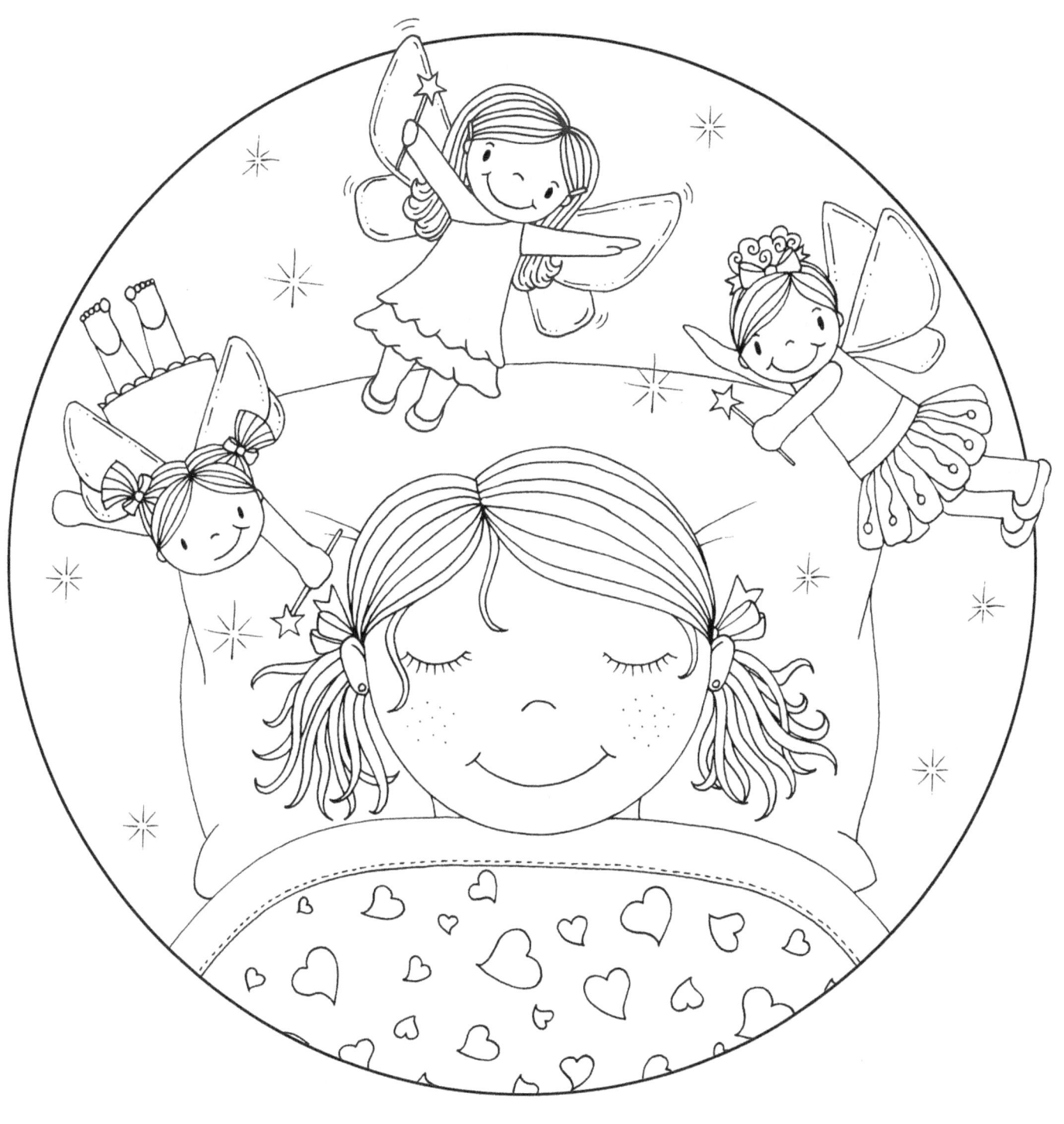

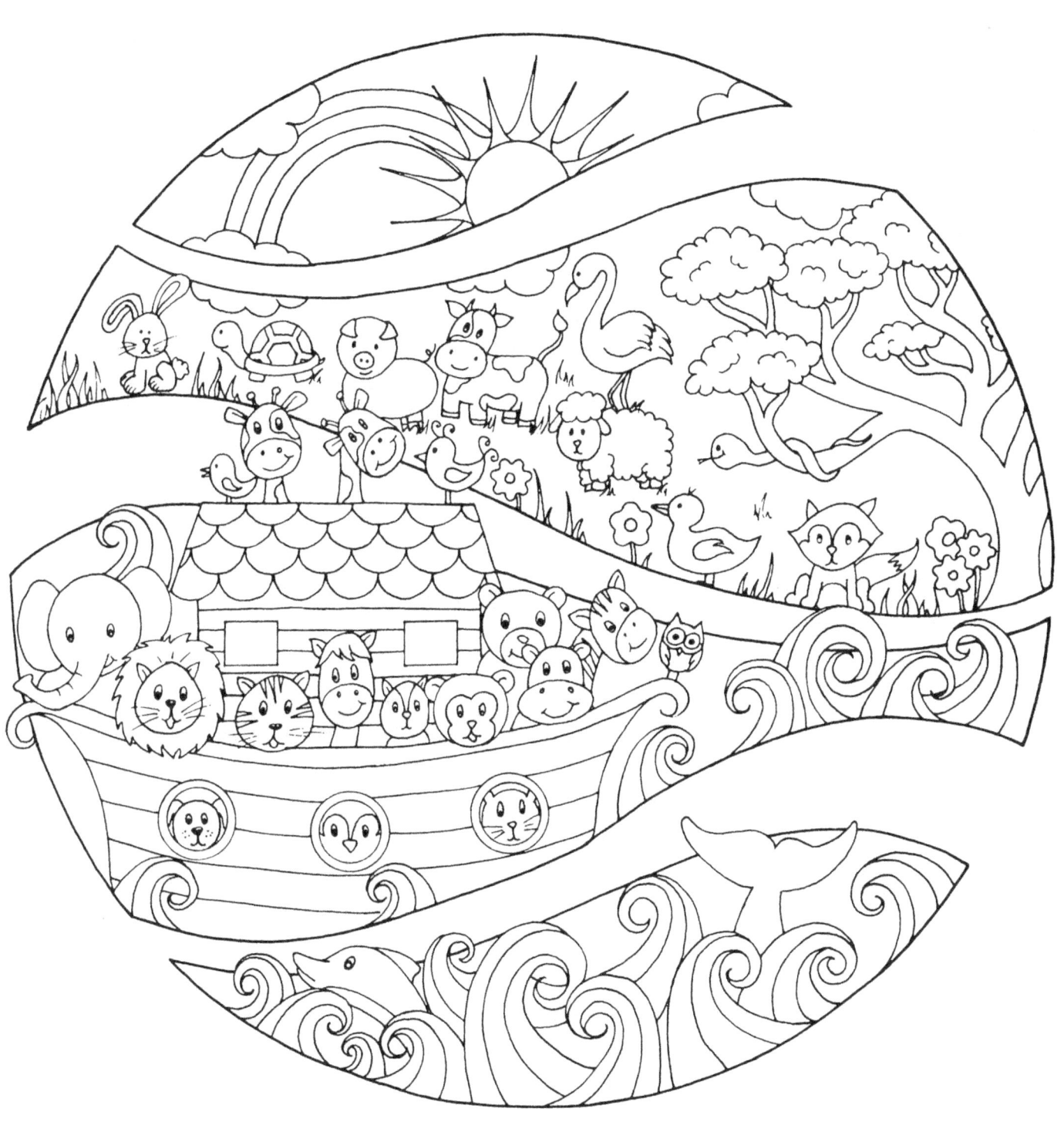

Broken Circles © 2019 Tabitha Barnett

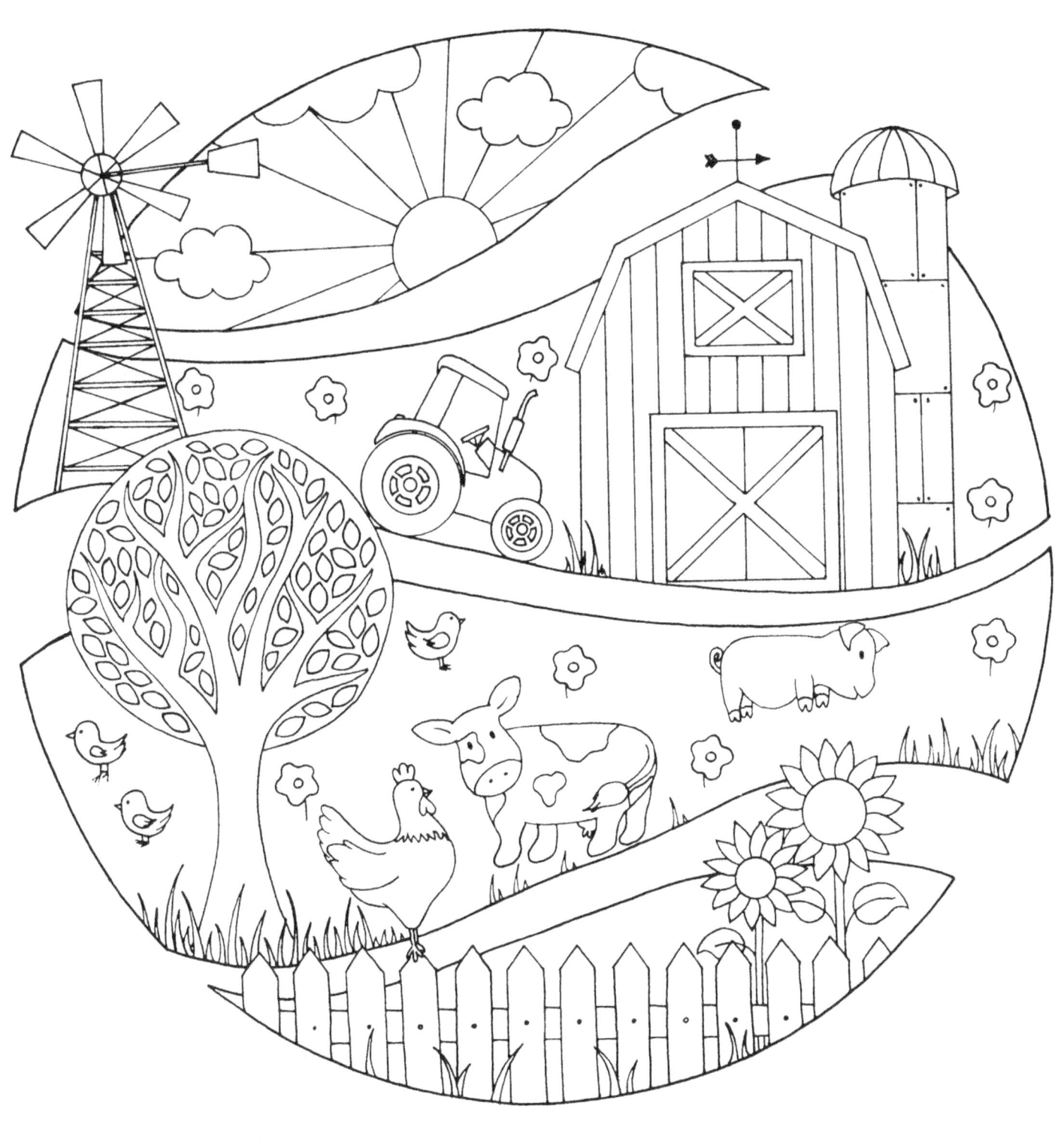

Broken Circles ©2019 Tabitha Barnett

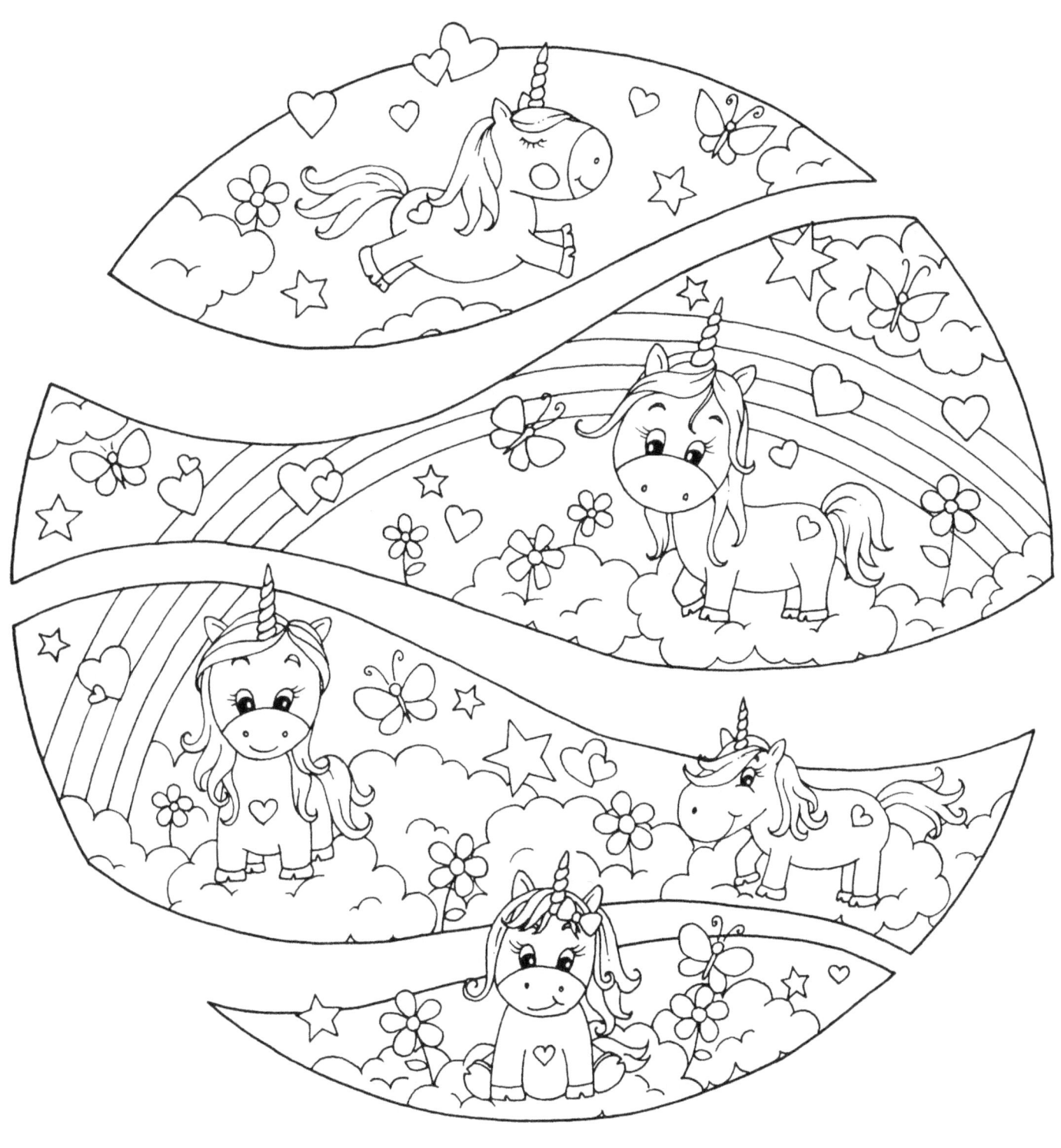
Broken Circles

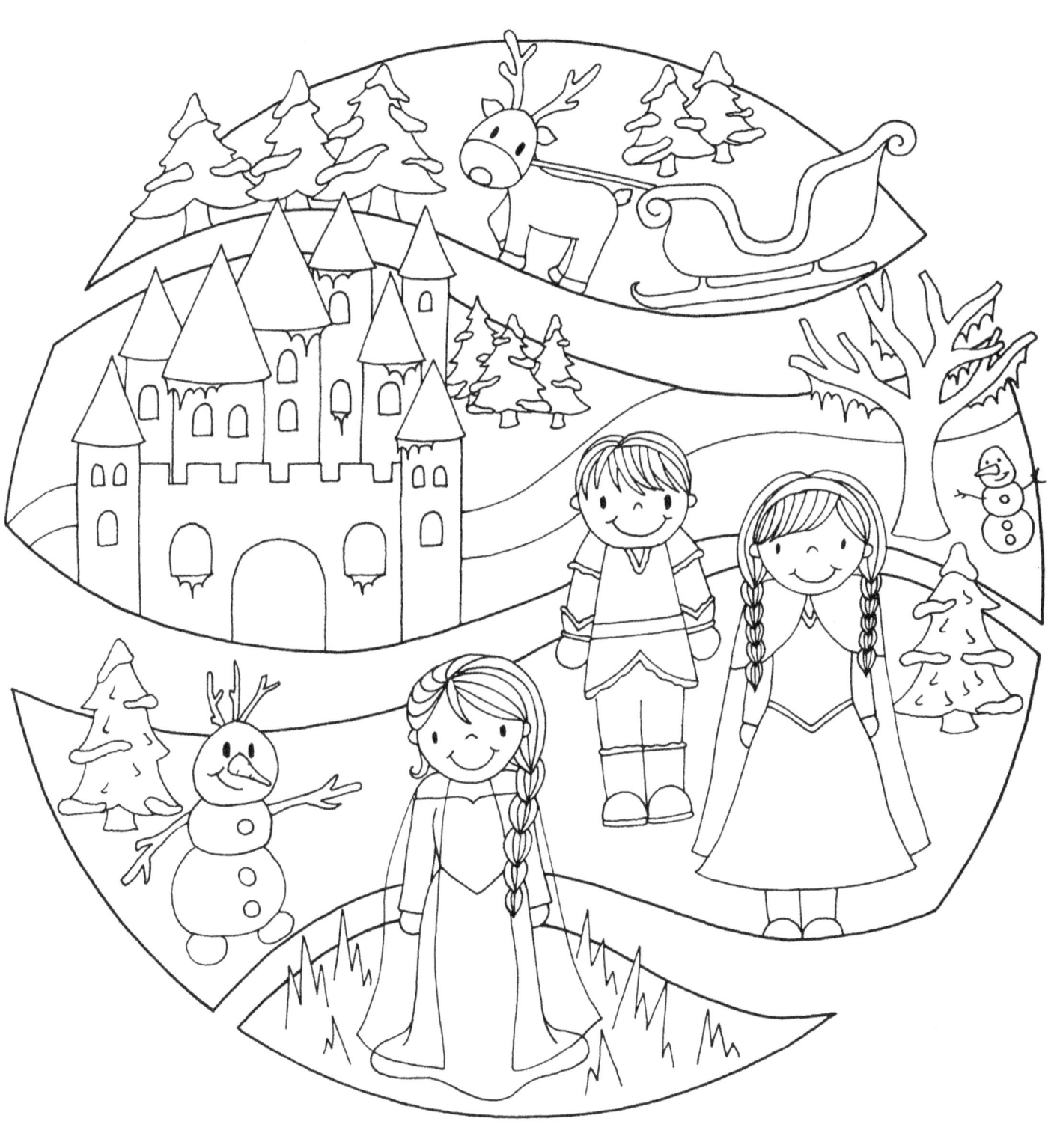

Broken Circles 2: A Fairy Tale Adventure ©2019 Tabitha Barnett

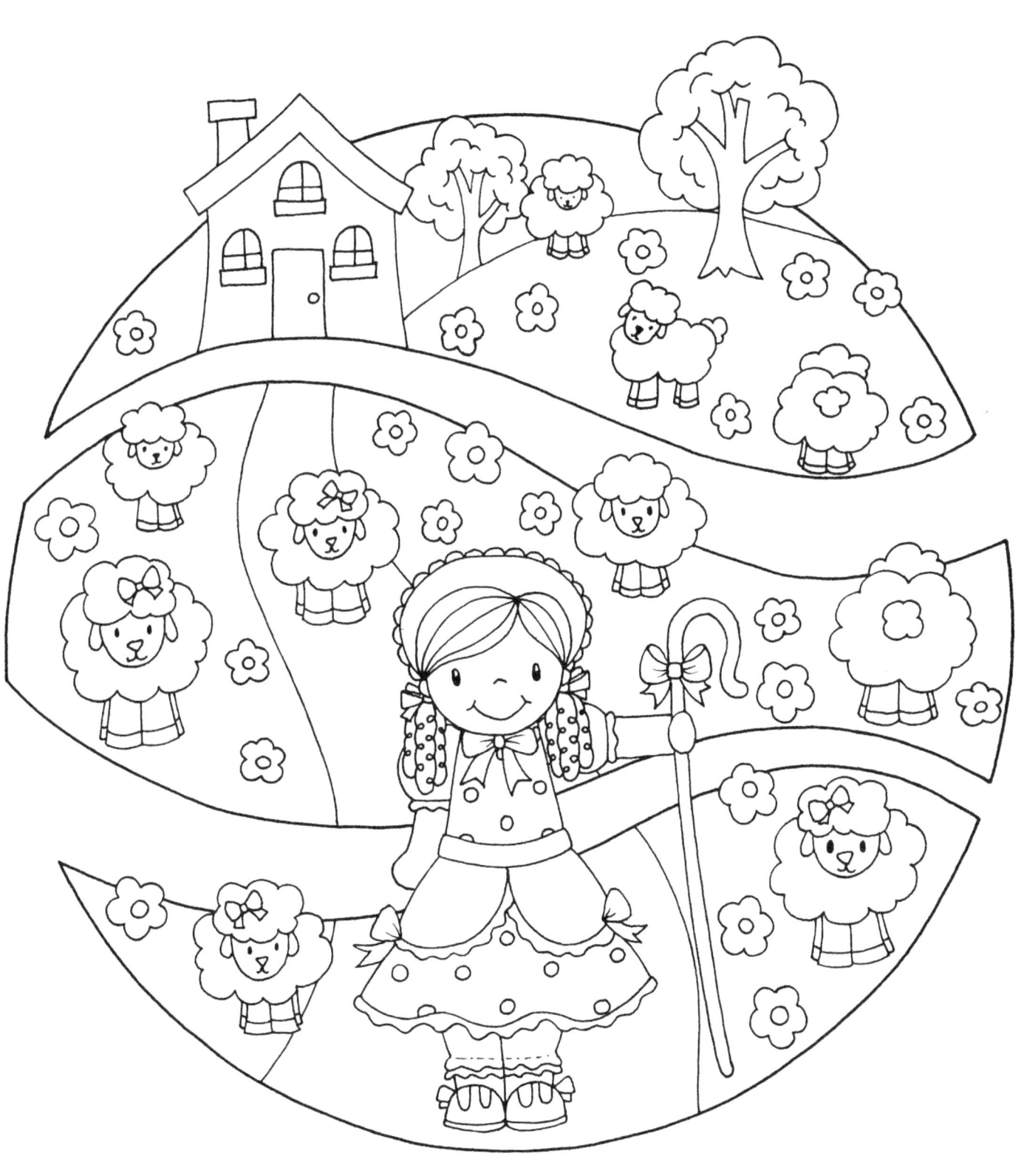

Broken Circles 2:   A Fairy Tale Adventure

©2019 Tabitha Barnett

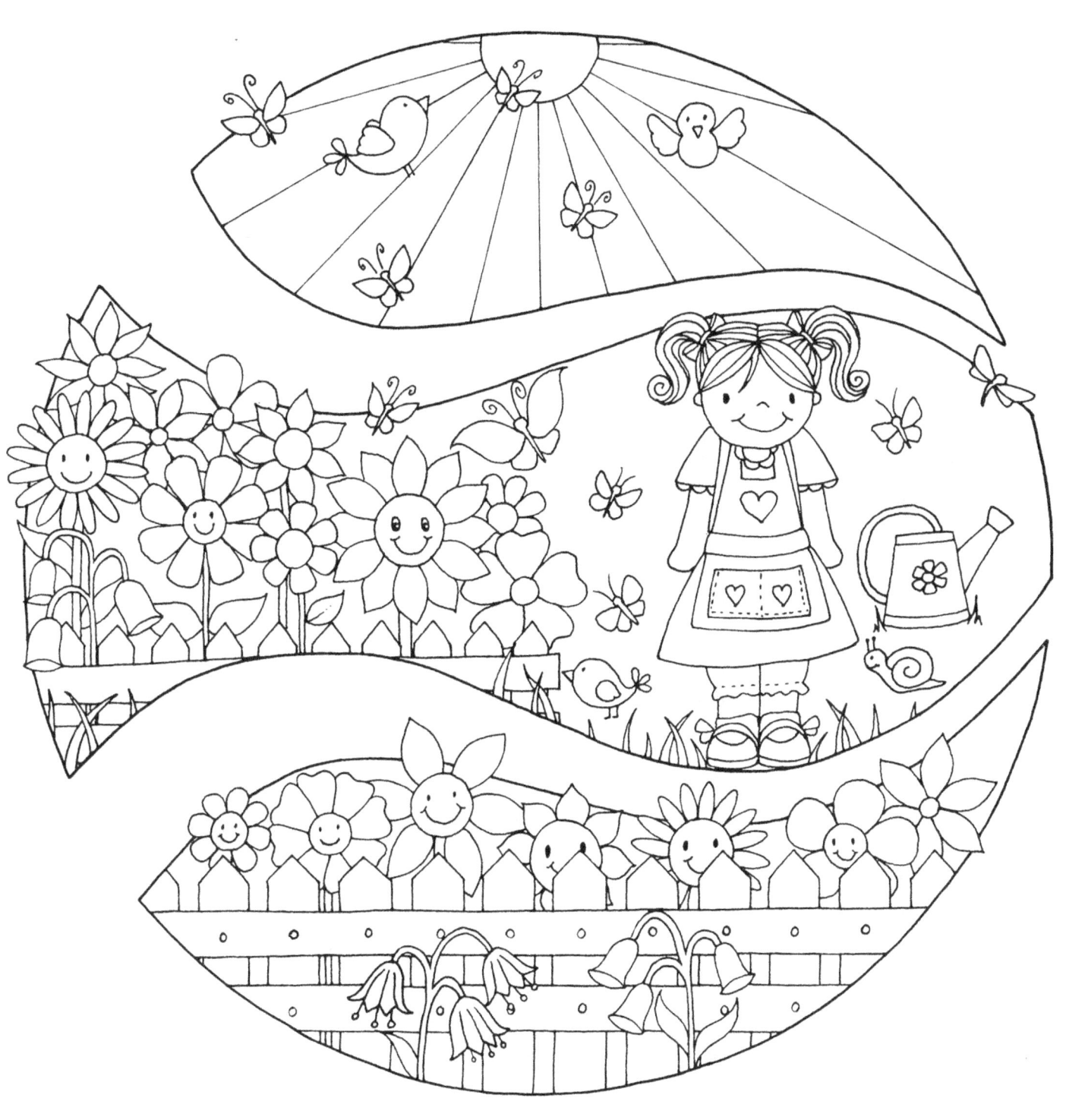

Broken Circles 2: A Fairy Tale Adventure ©2019 Tabitha Barnett

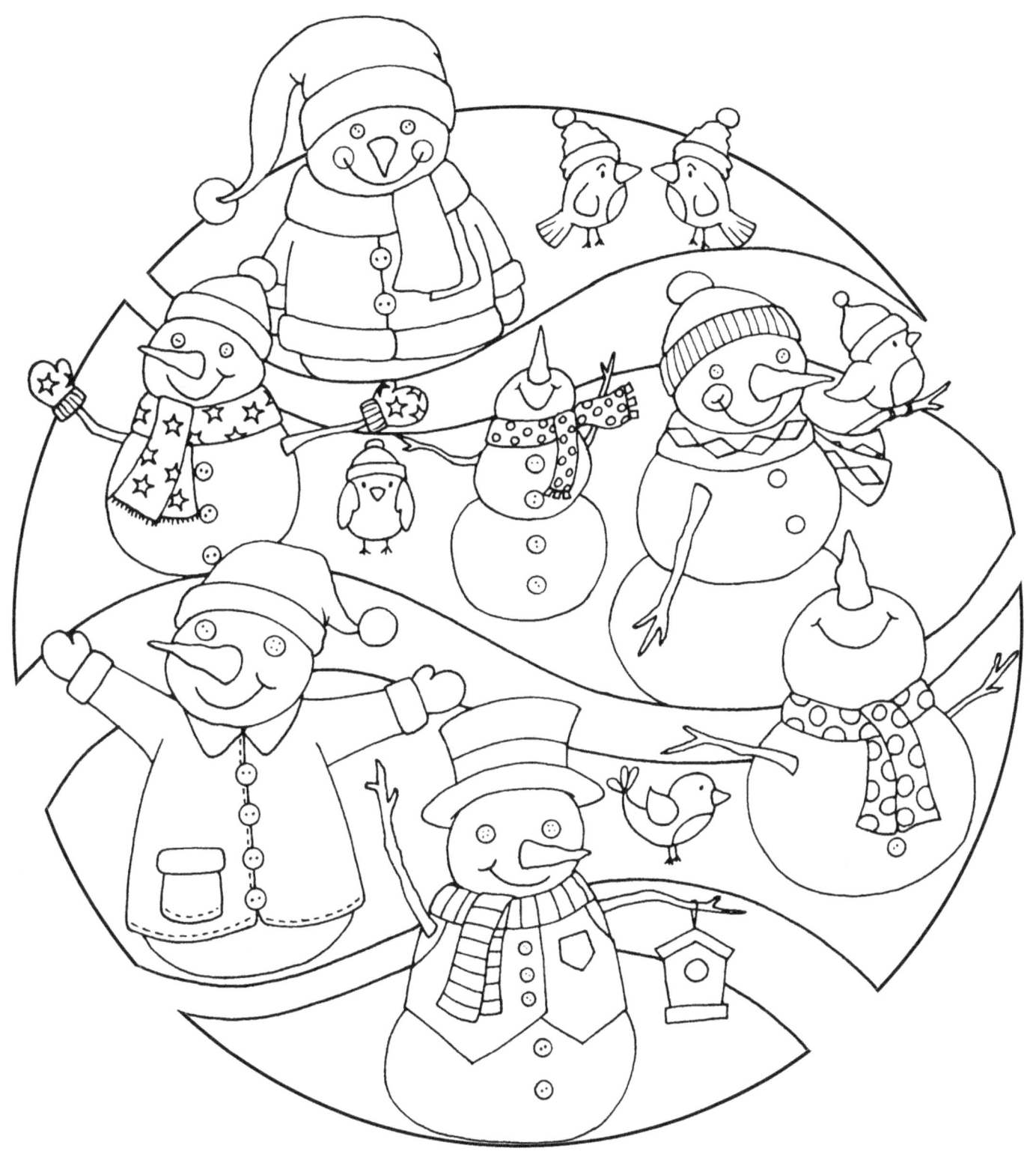

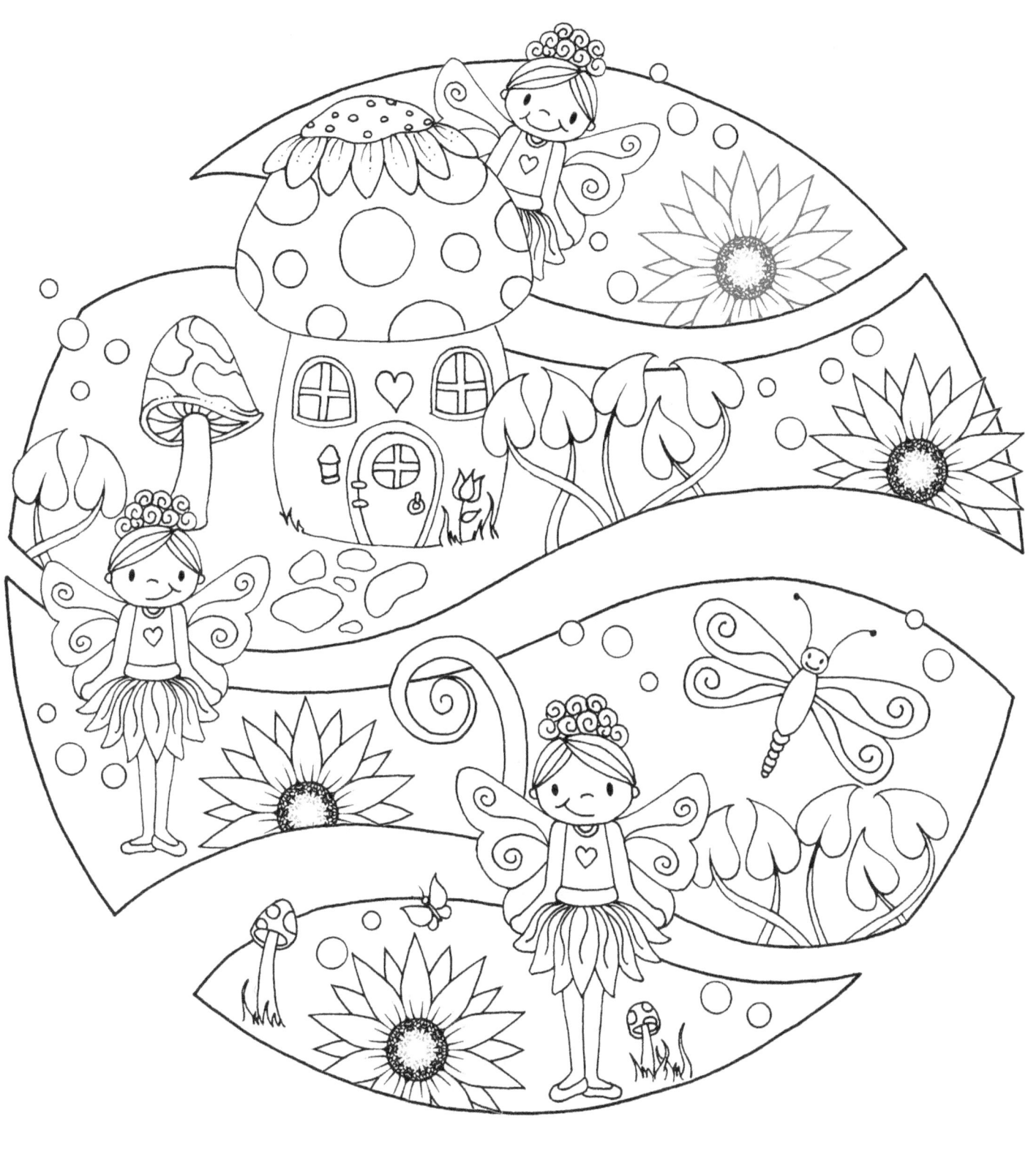

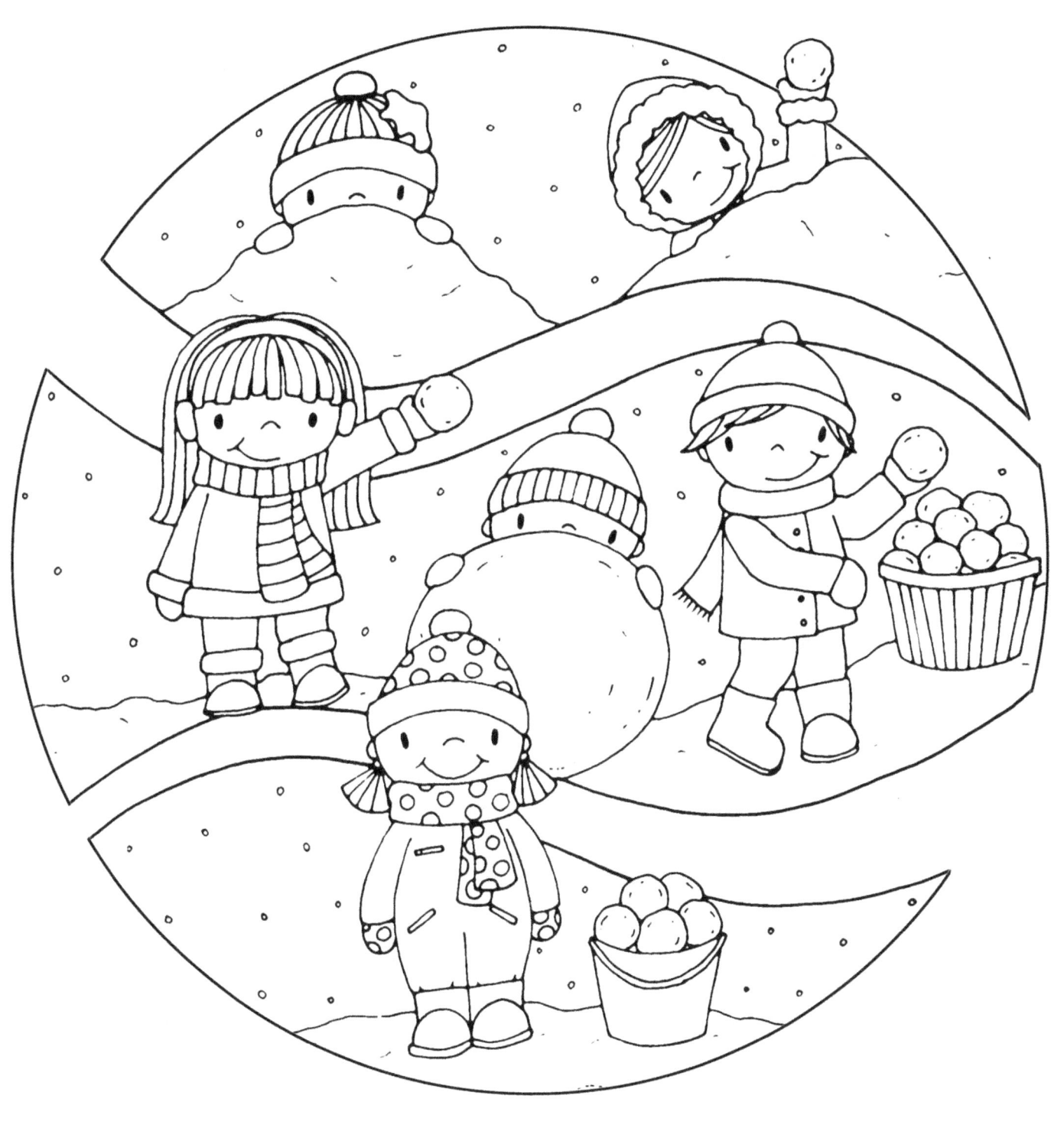

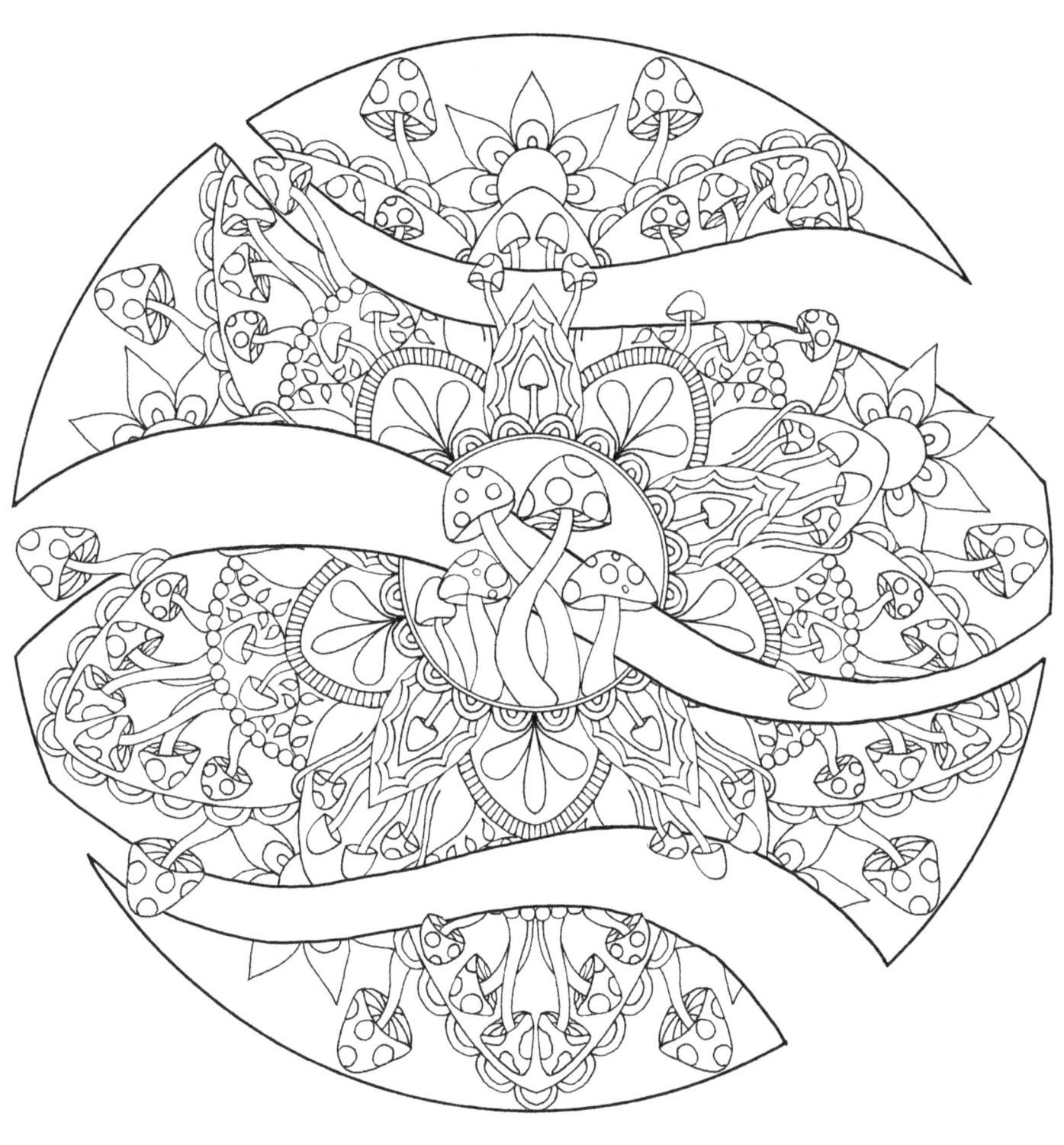

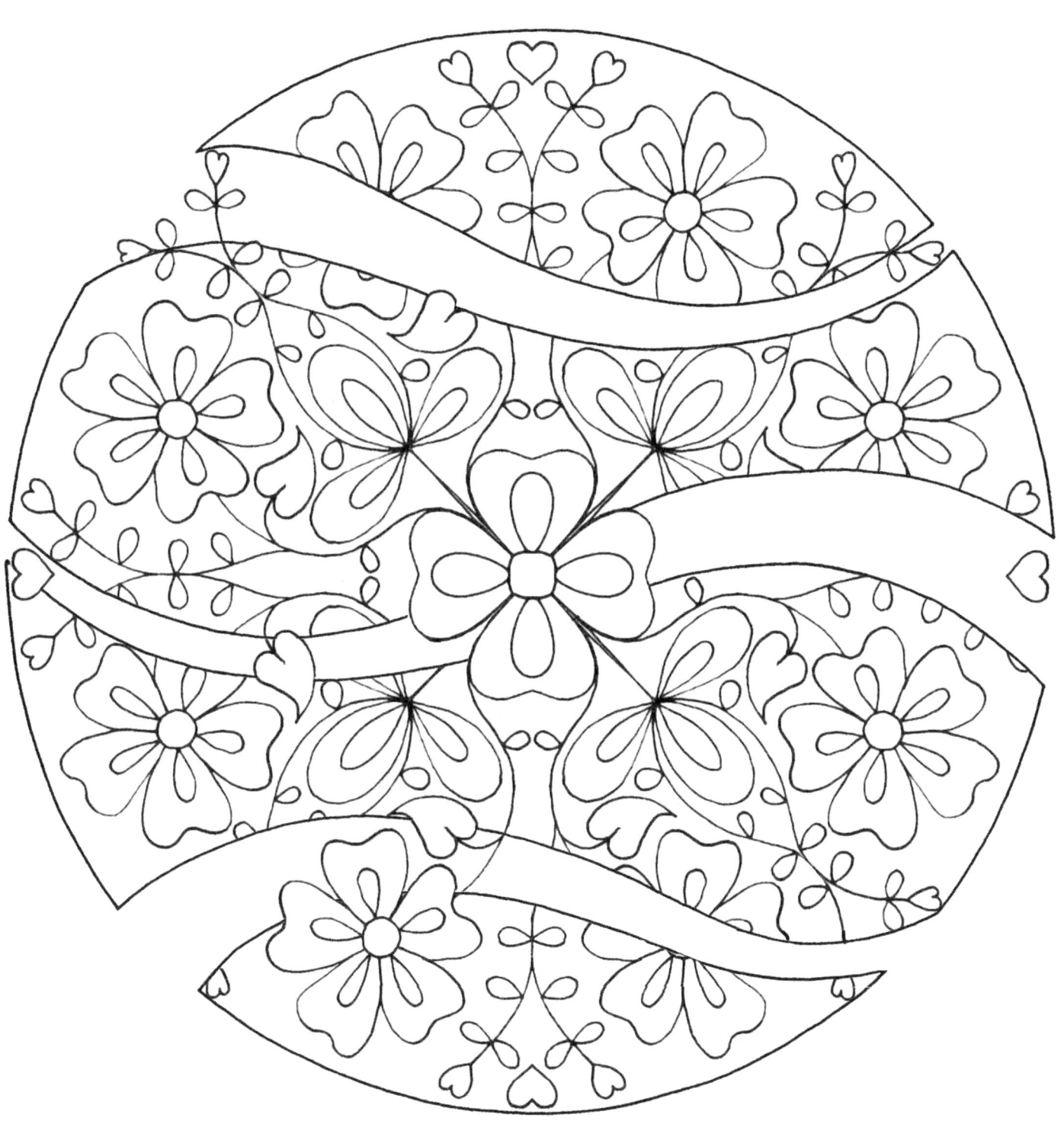

Broken Mandalas ©2019 Tabitha Barnett

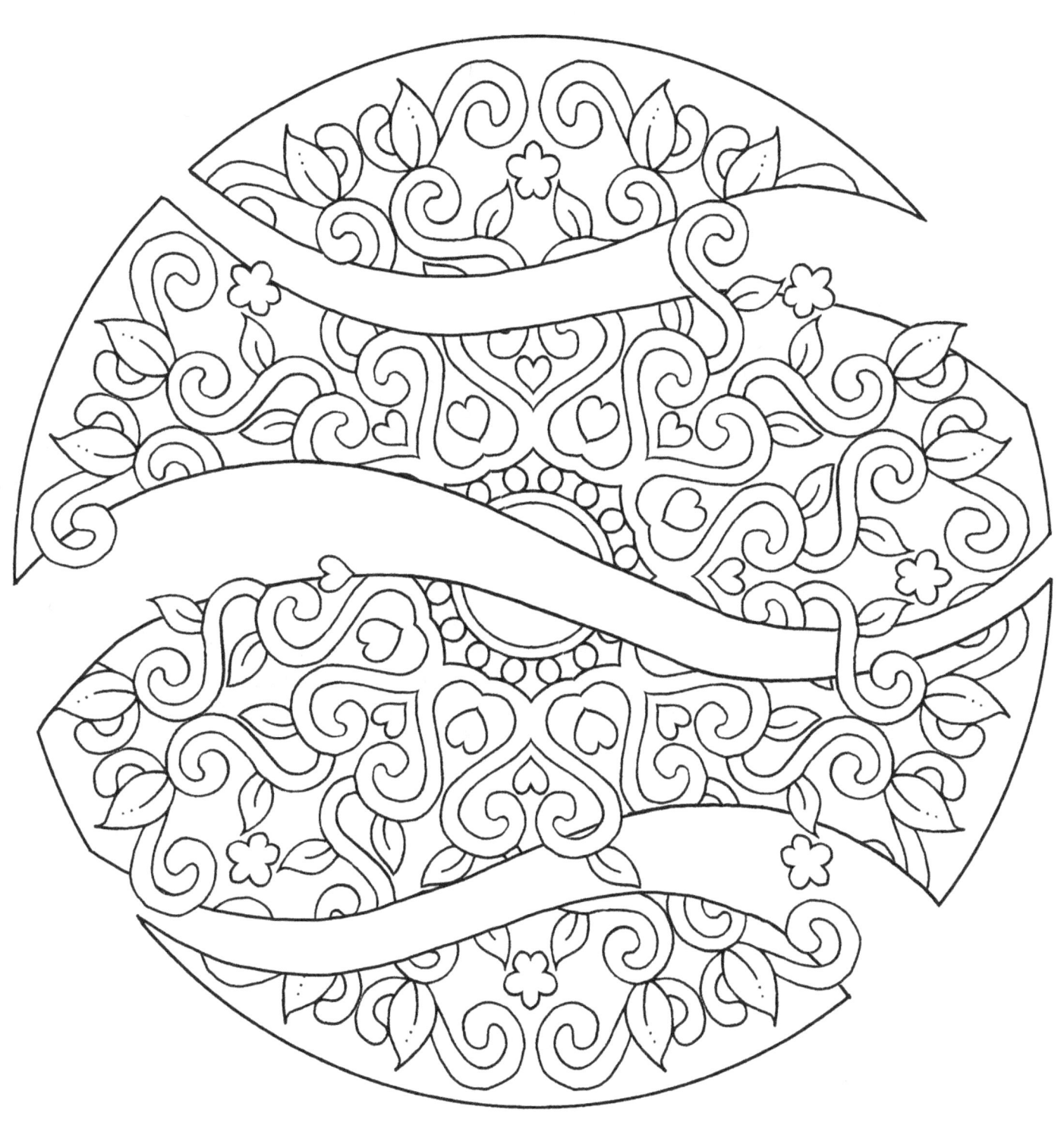

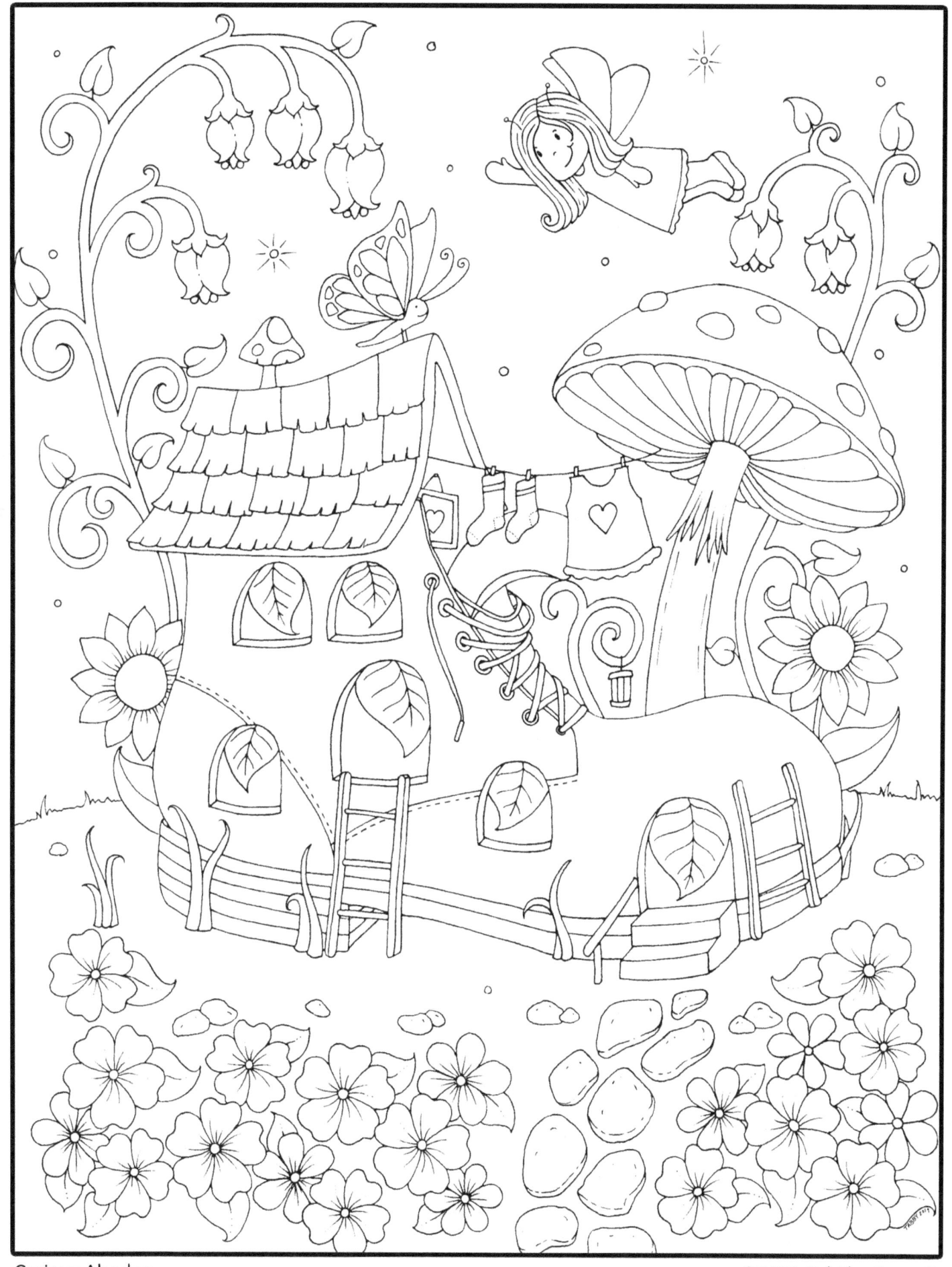

Curious Abodes © 2019 Tabitha Barnett

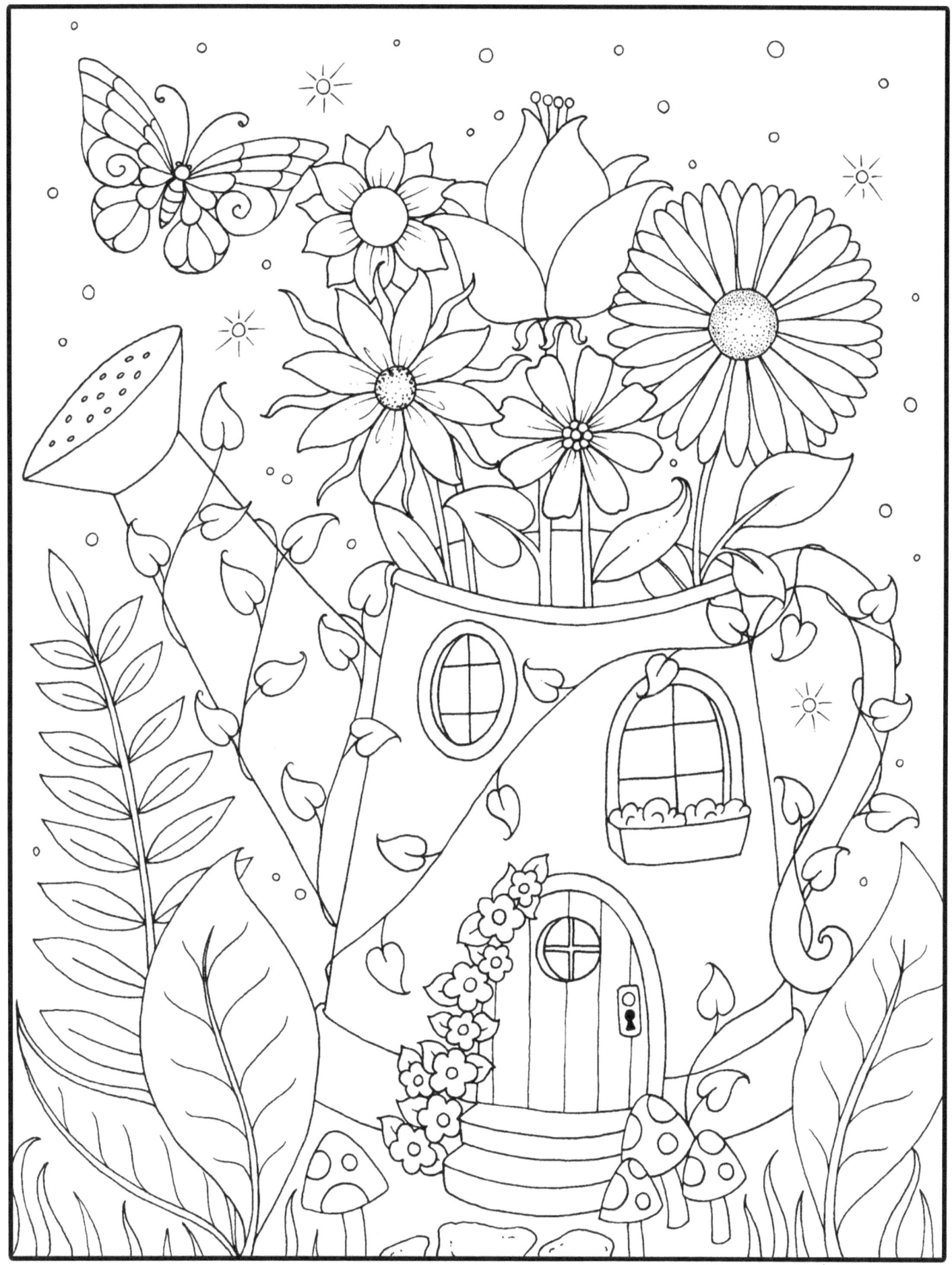

Curious Abodes ©2019 Tabitha Barnett

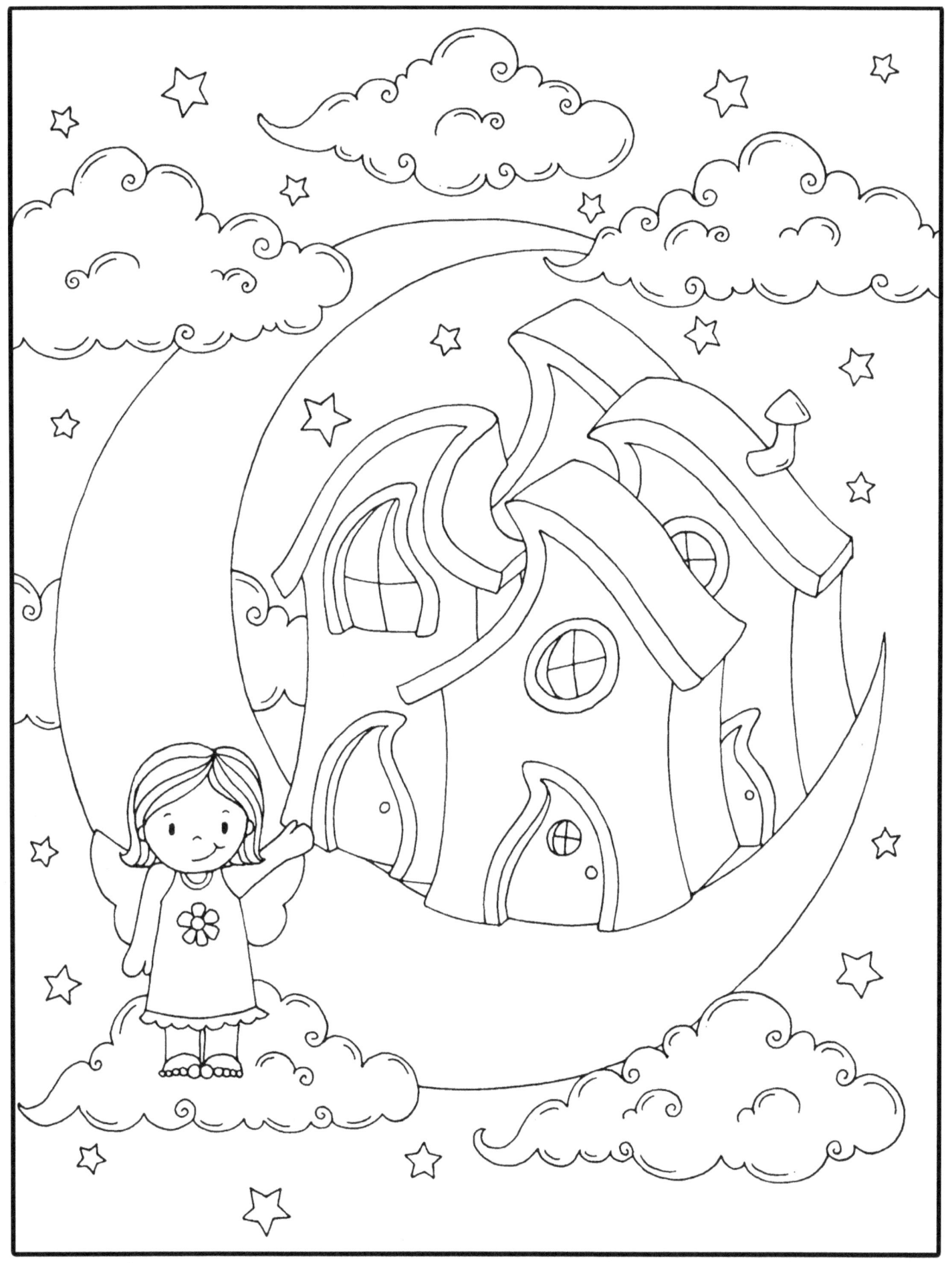

Curious Abodes ©2019 Tabitha Barnett

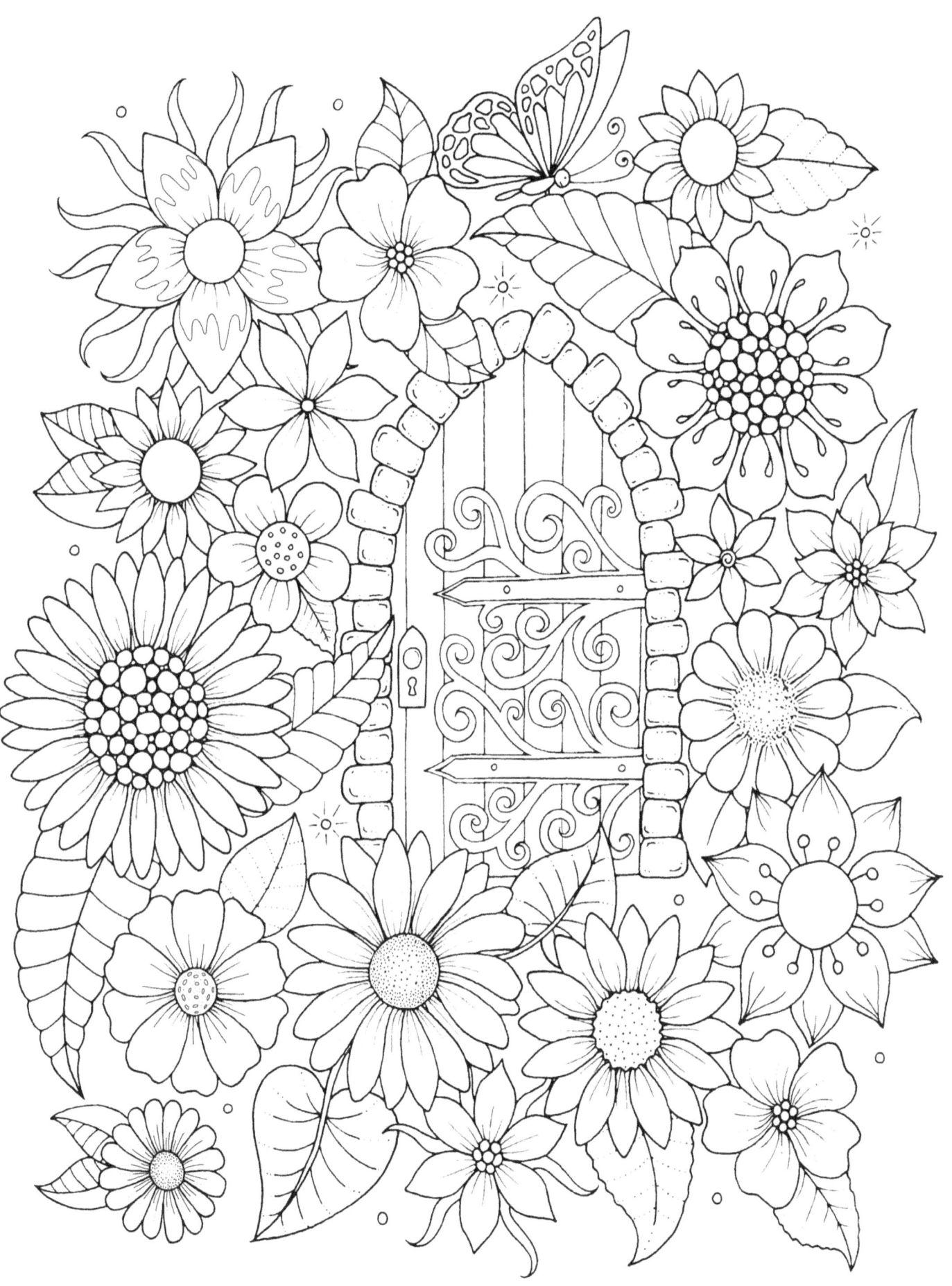

Curious Abodes © 2019 Tabitha Barnett

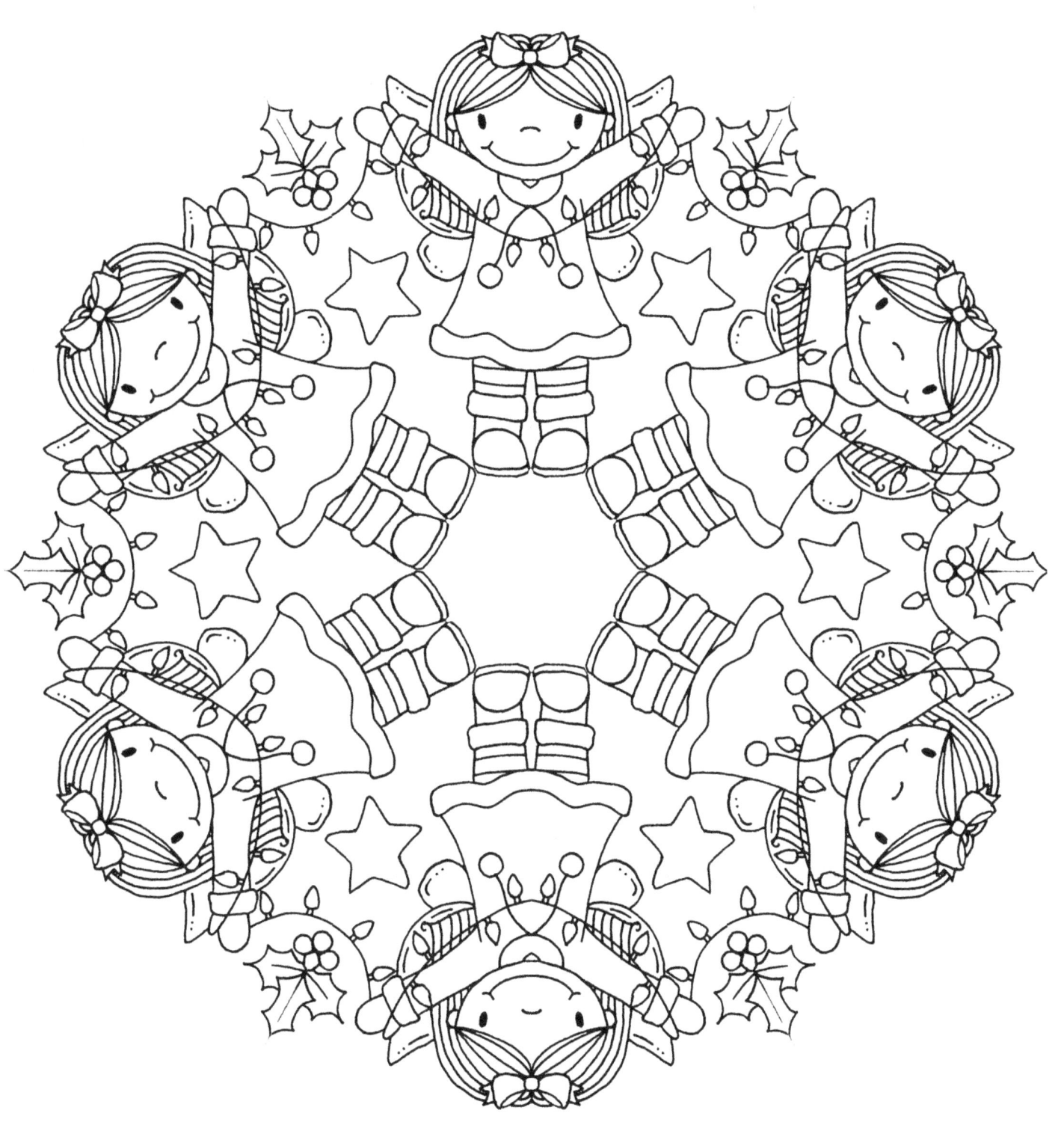

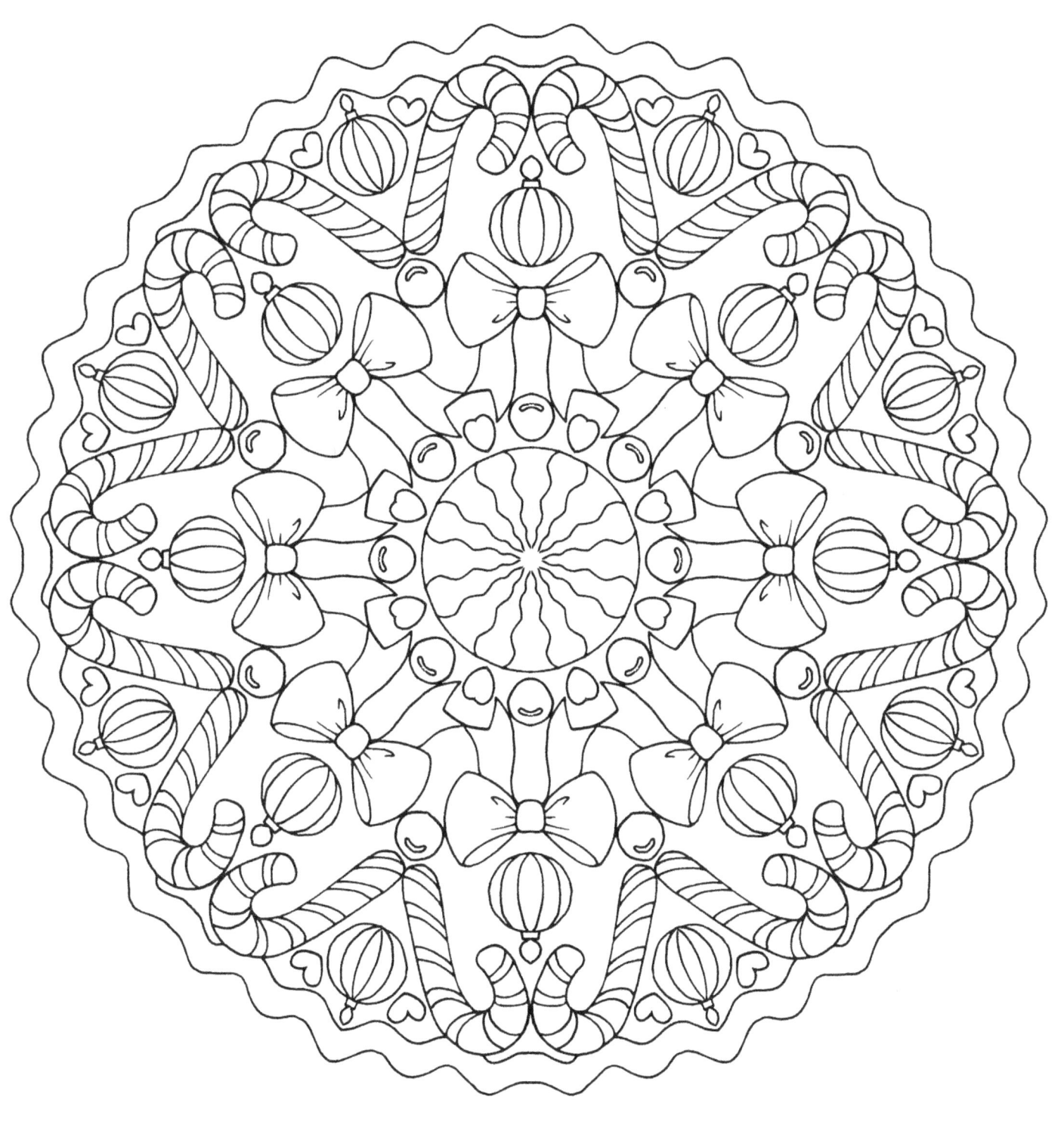

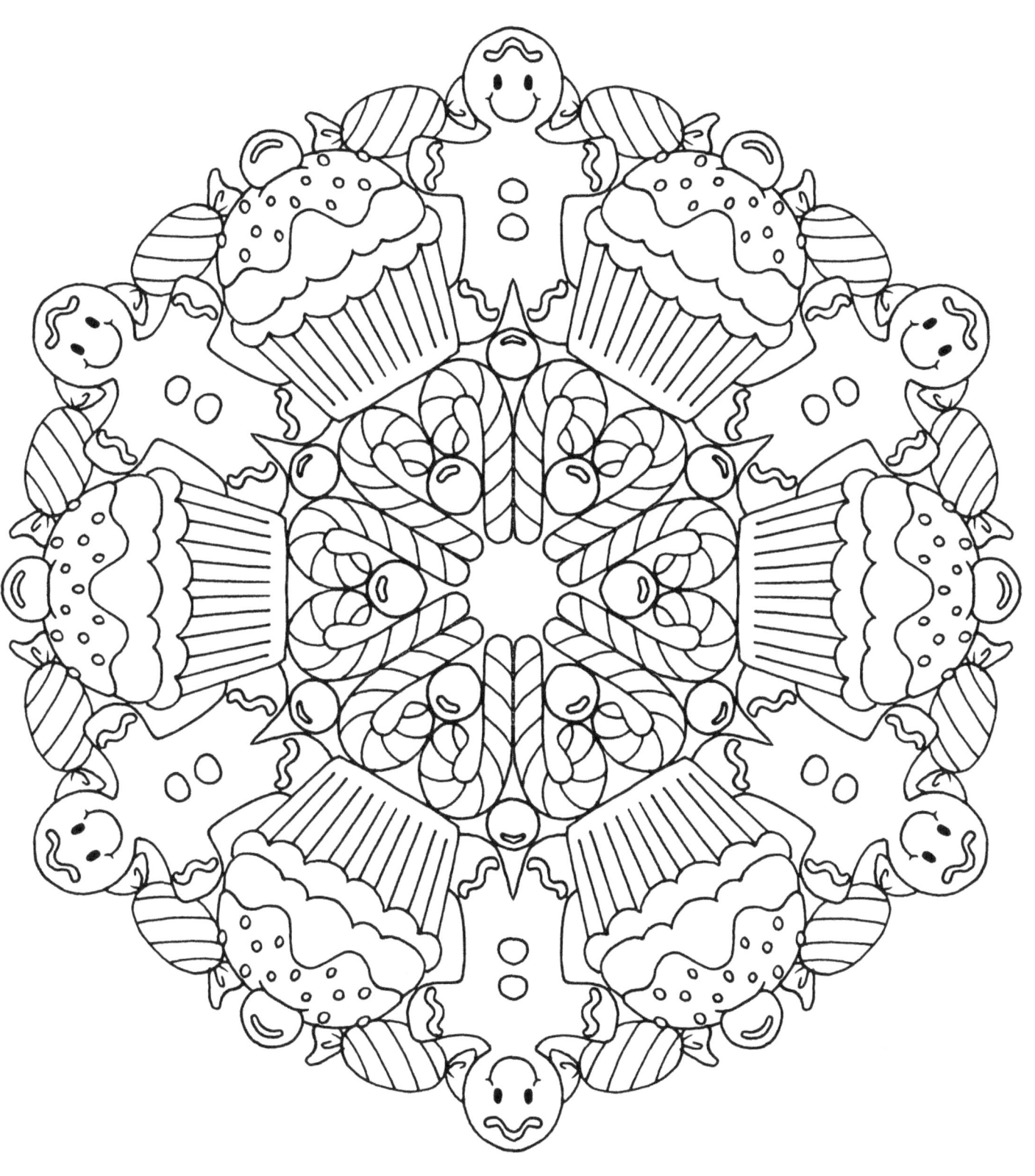

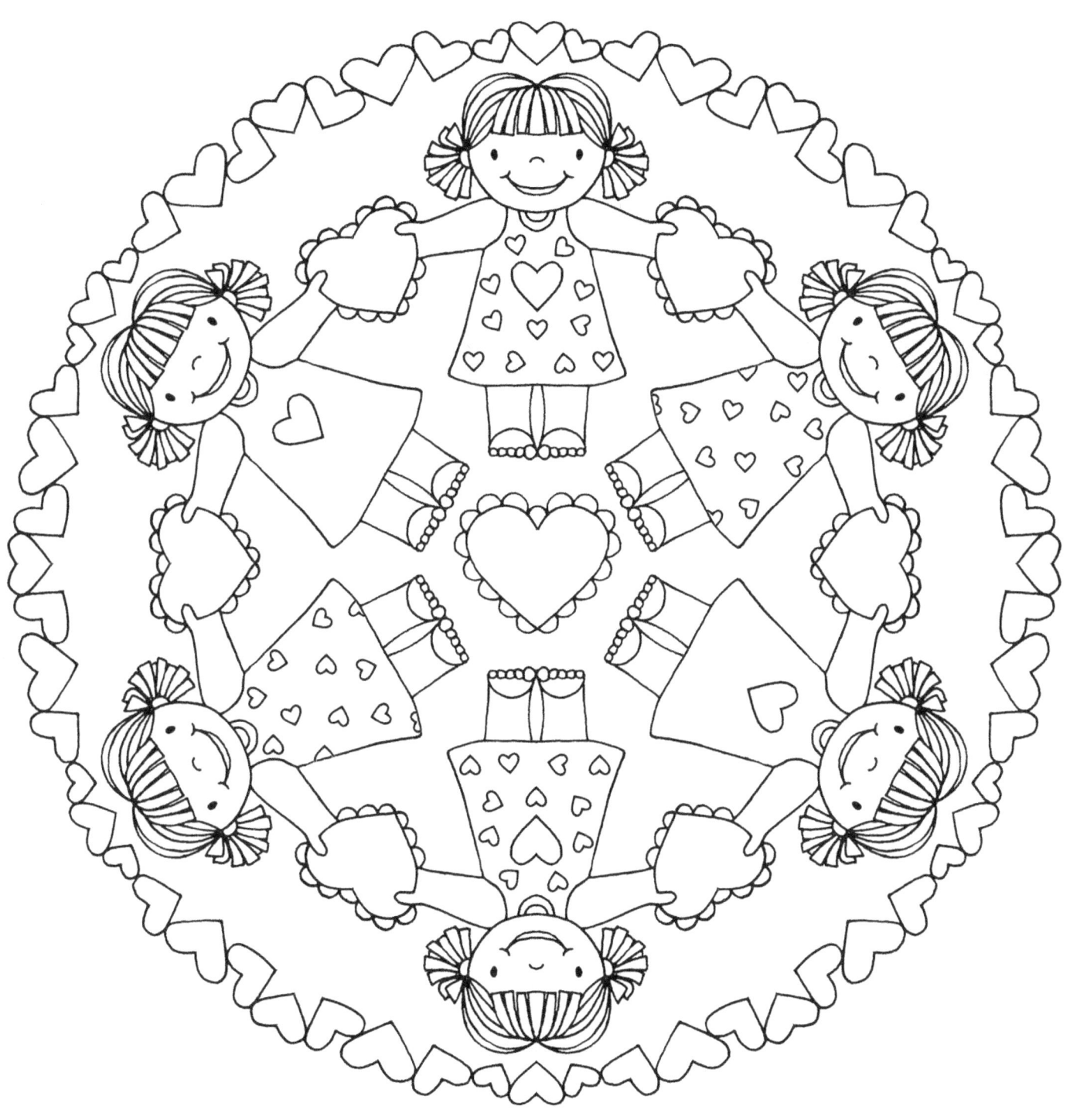

Circles of Love

©2019 Tabitha Barnett

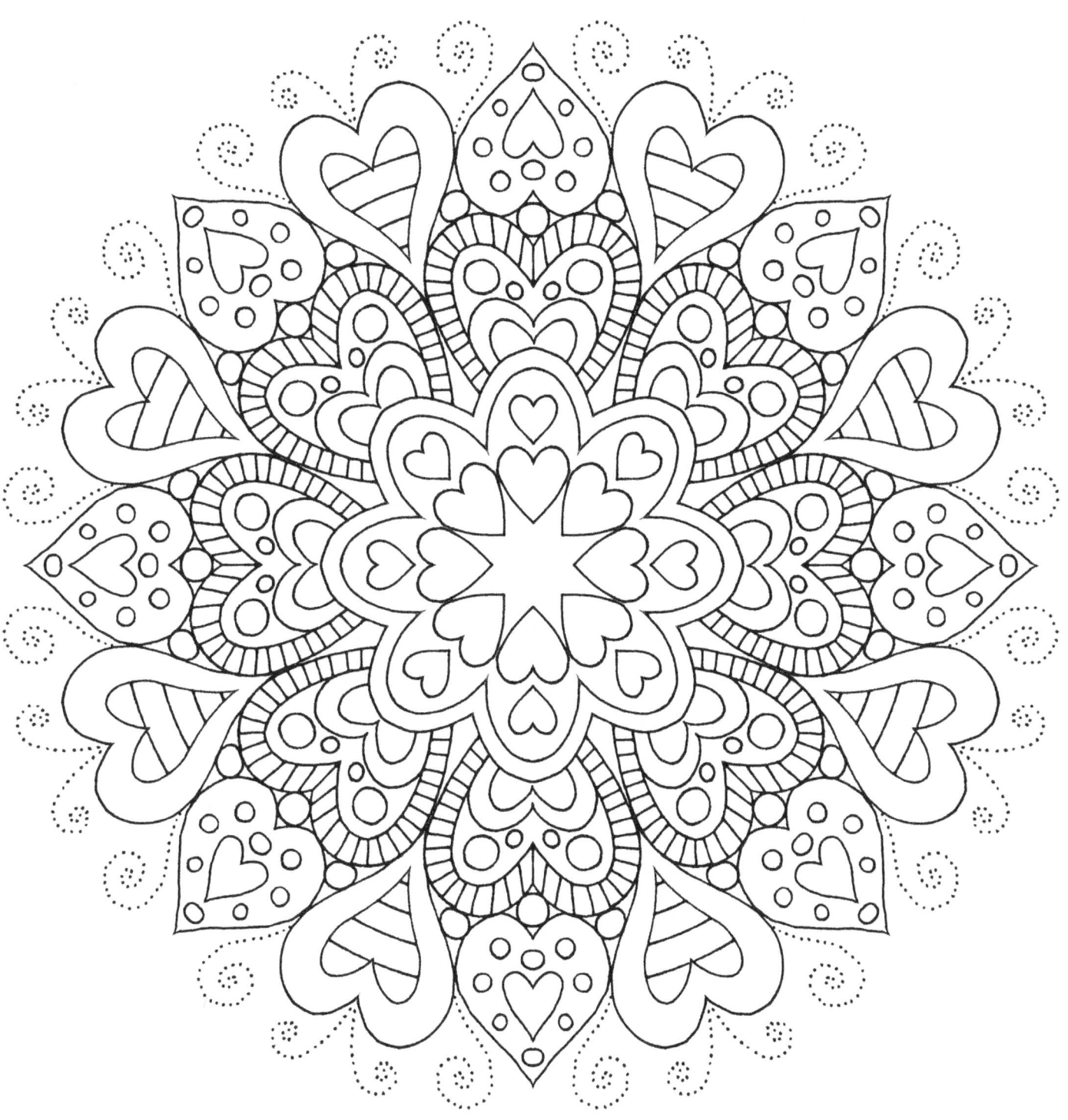

Circles of Love ©2019 Tabitha Barnett

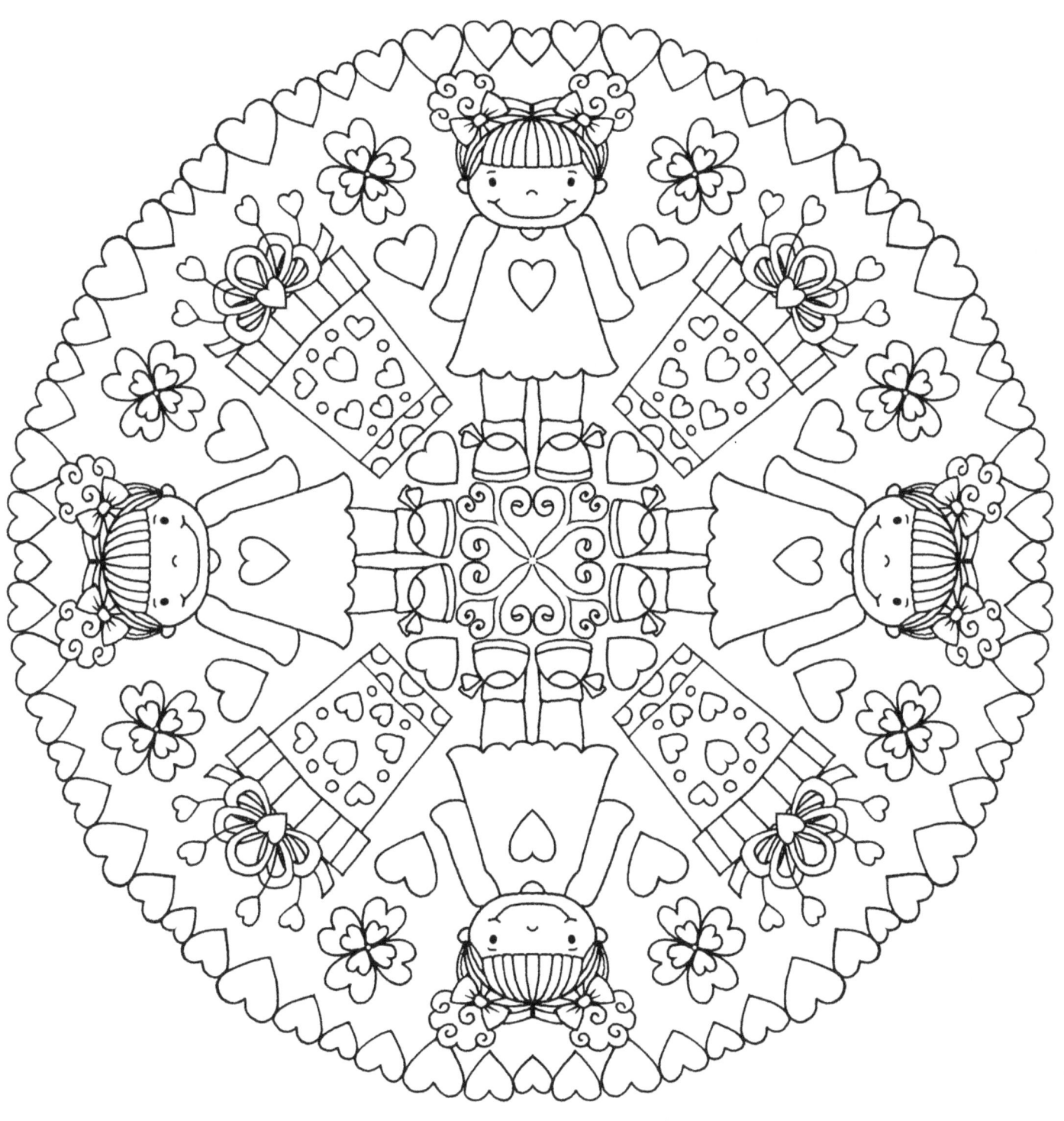

Circles of Love ©2019 Tabitha Barnett

Circles of Love

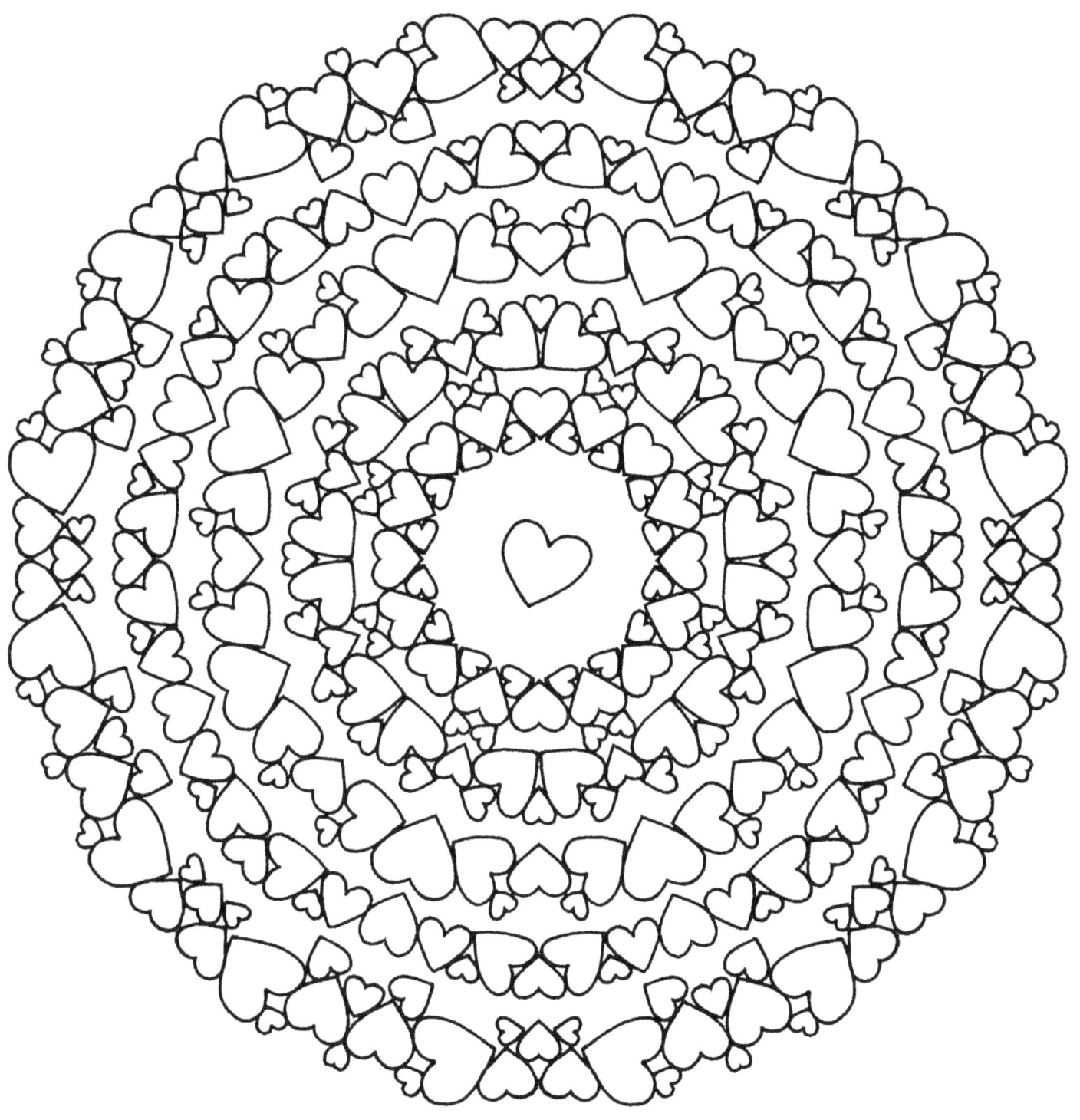

©2019 Tabitha Barnett

It's Fall, Y'All

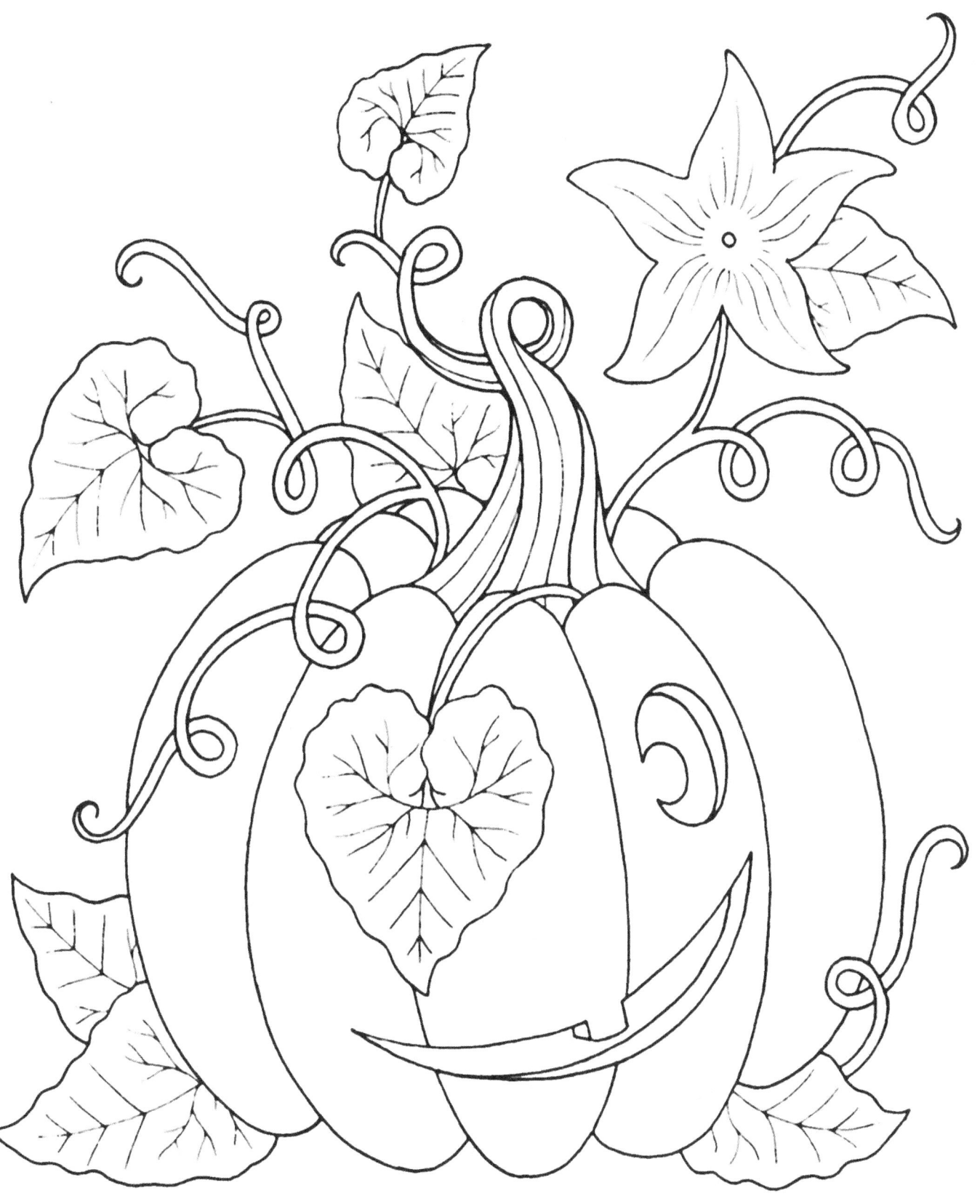

©2019 Tabitha Barnett

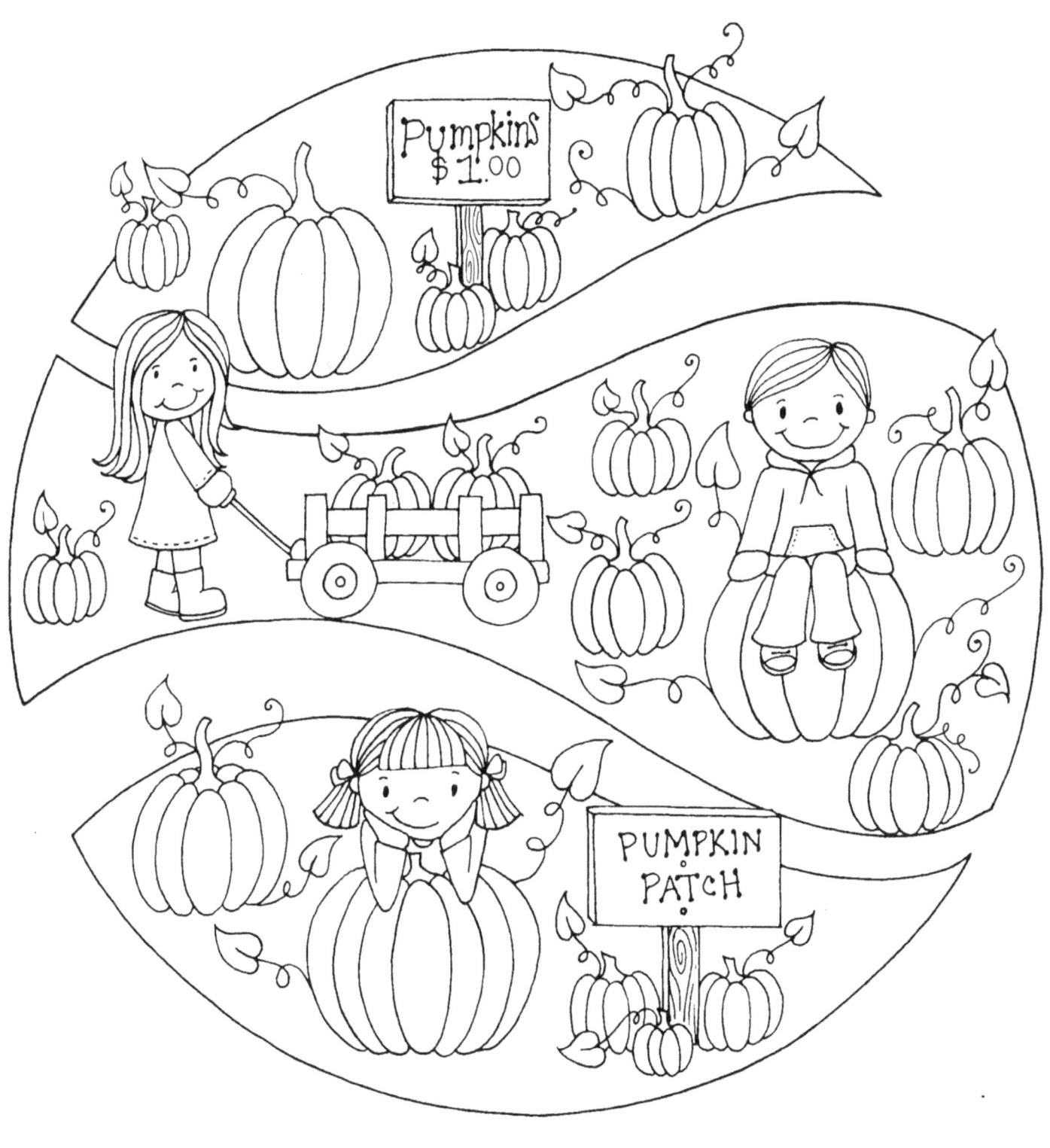

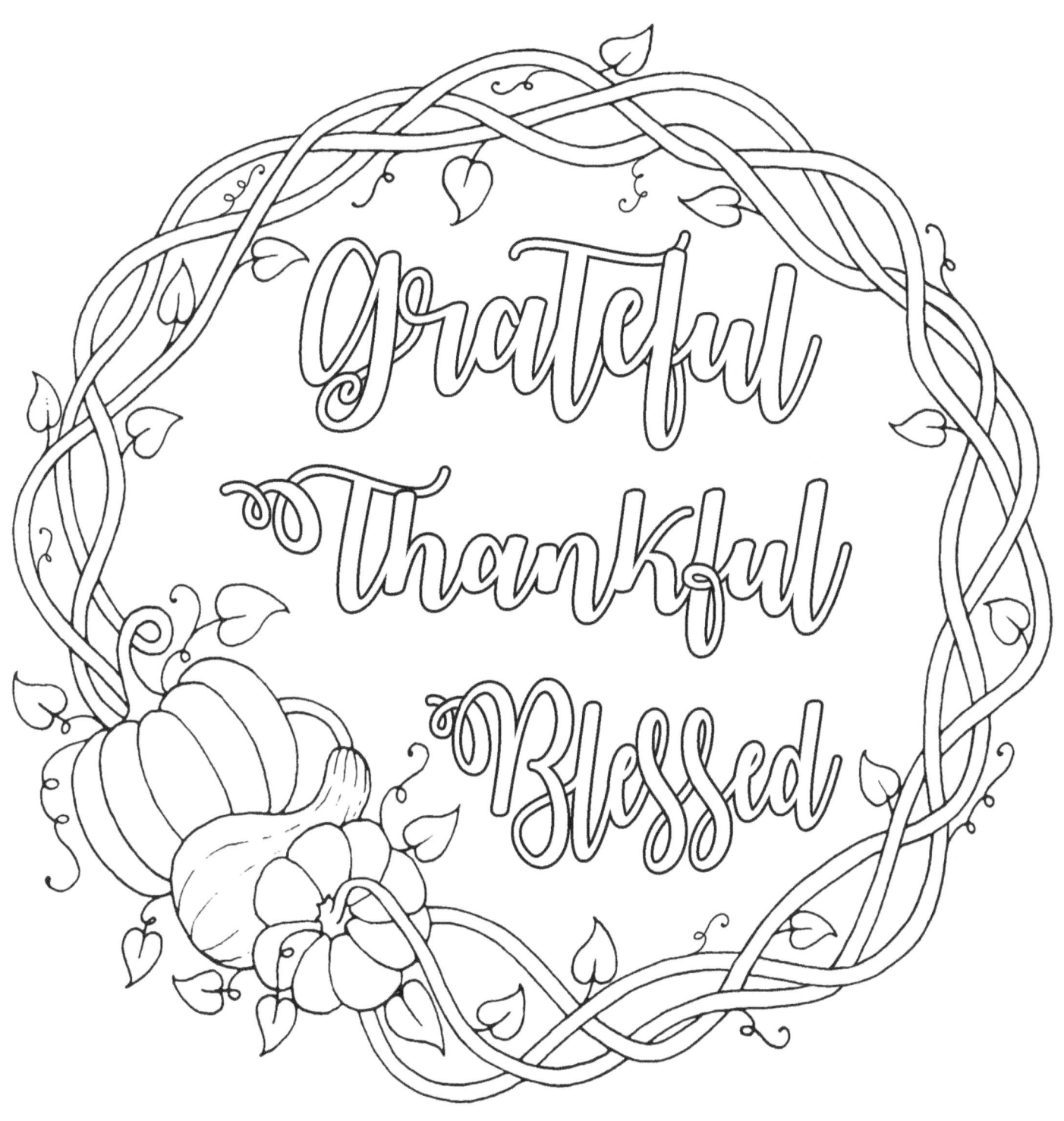

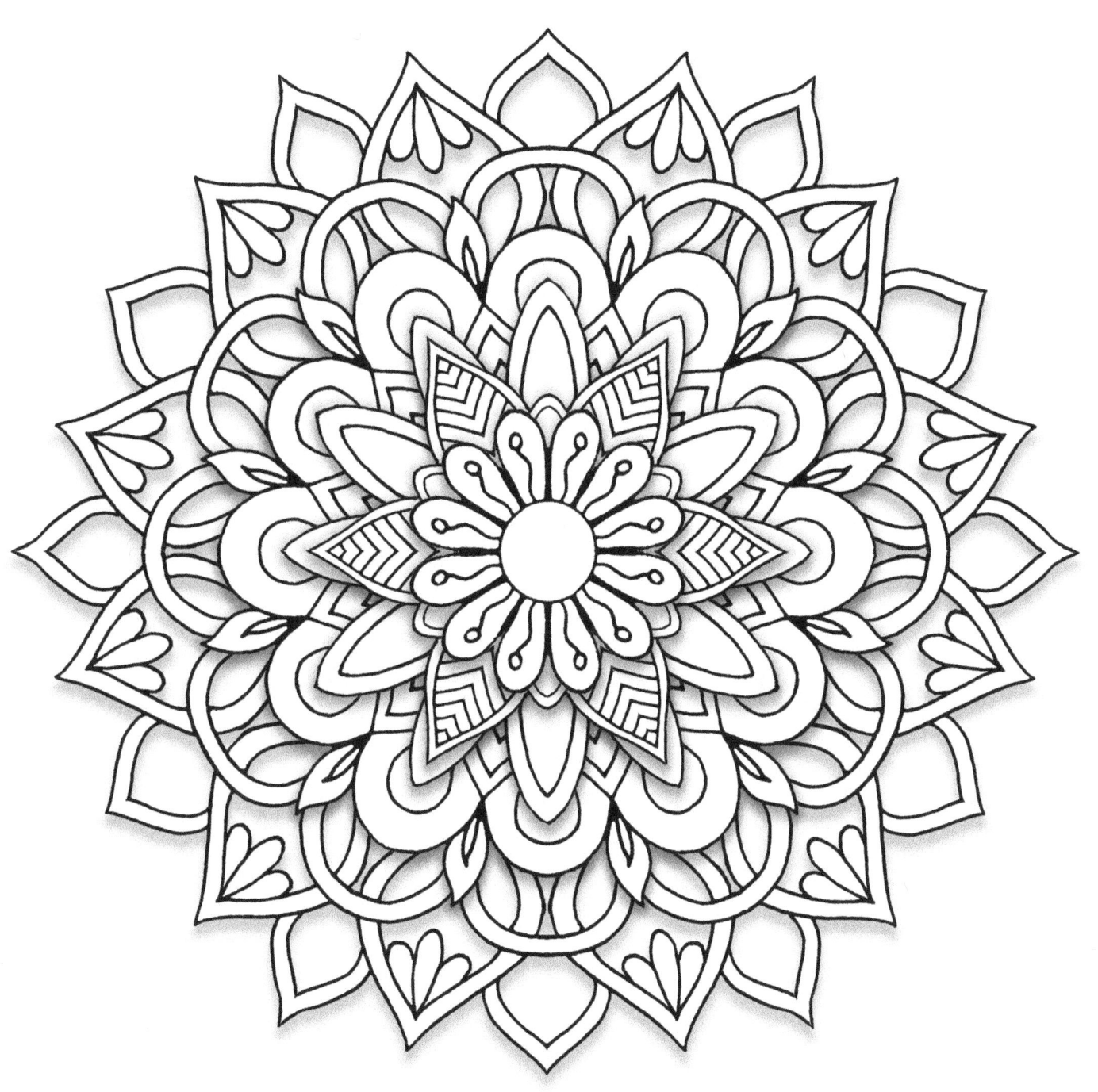

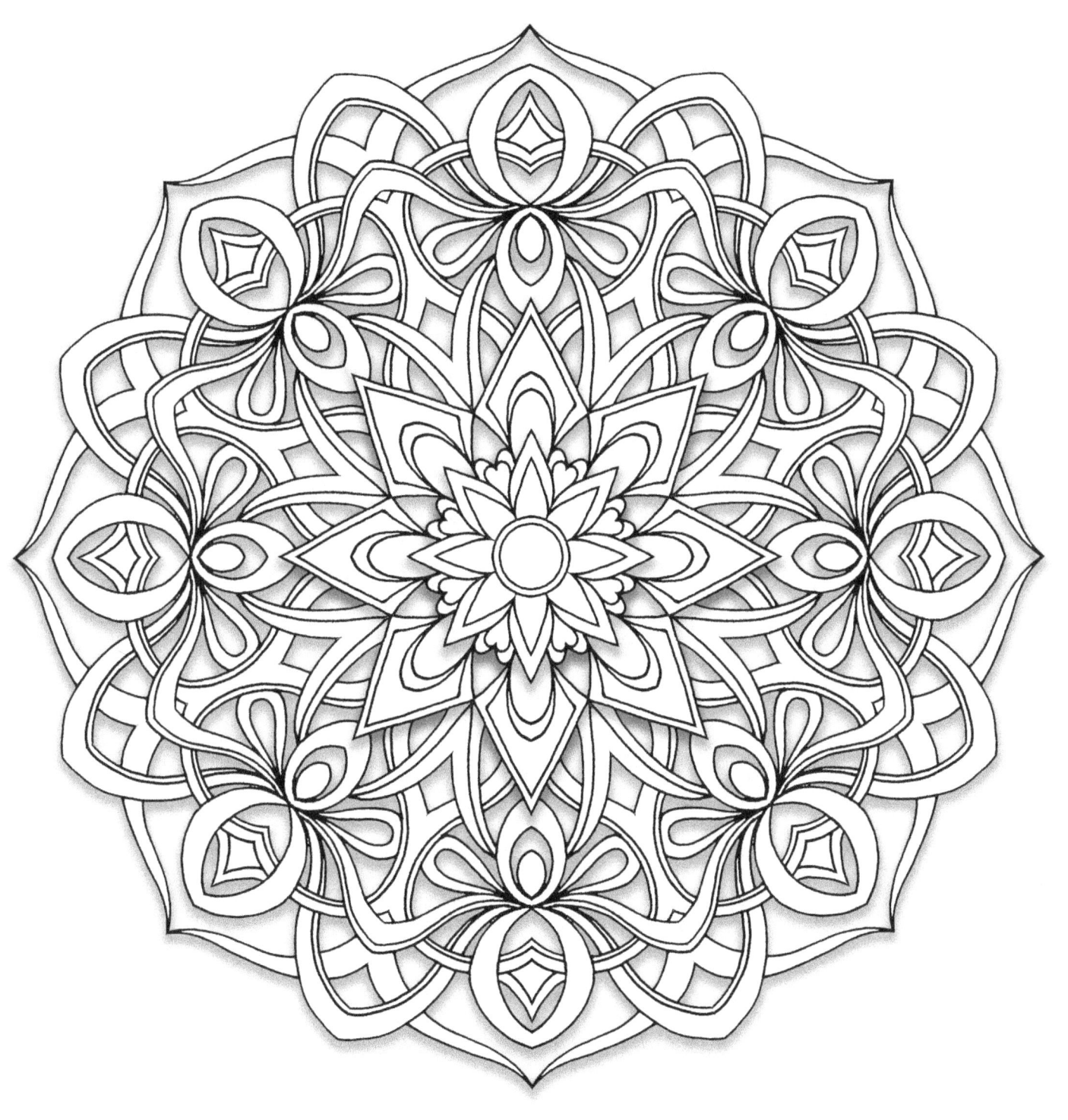

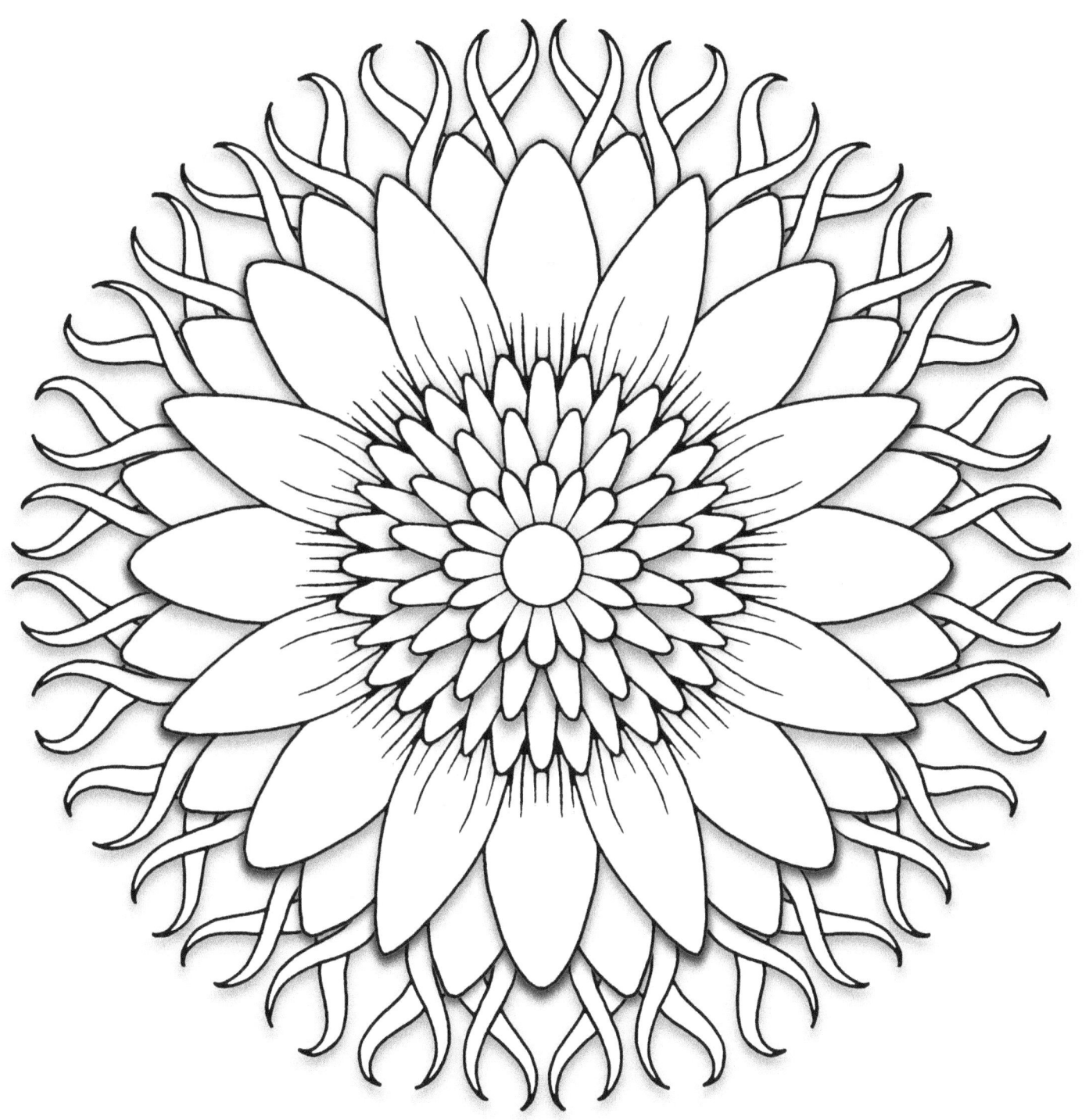

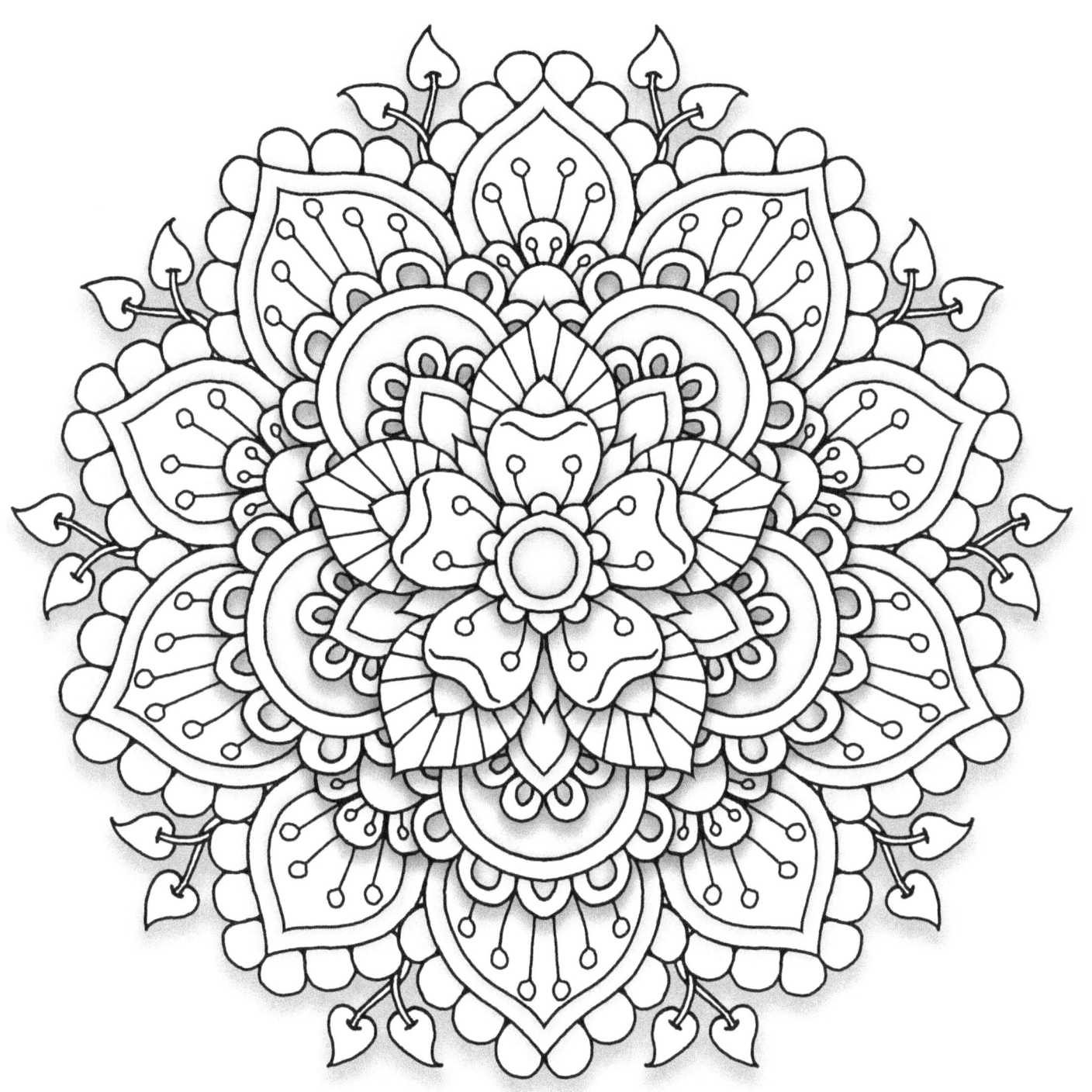

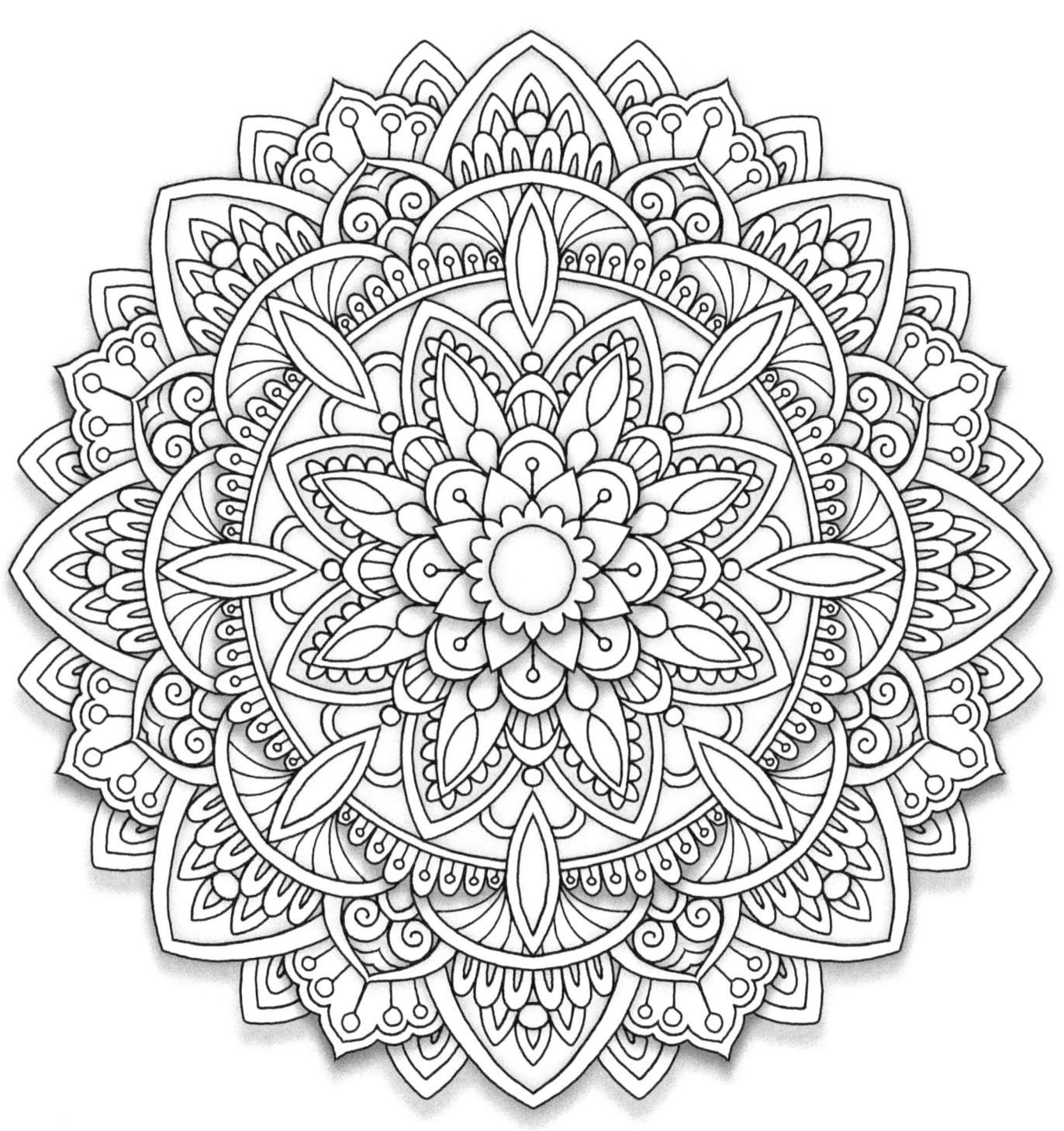

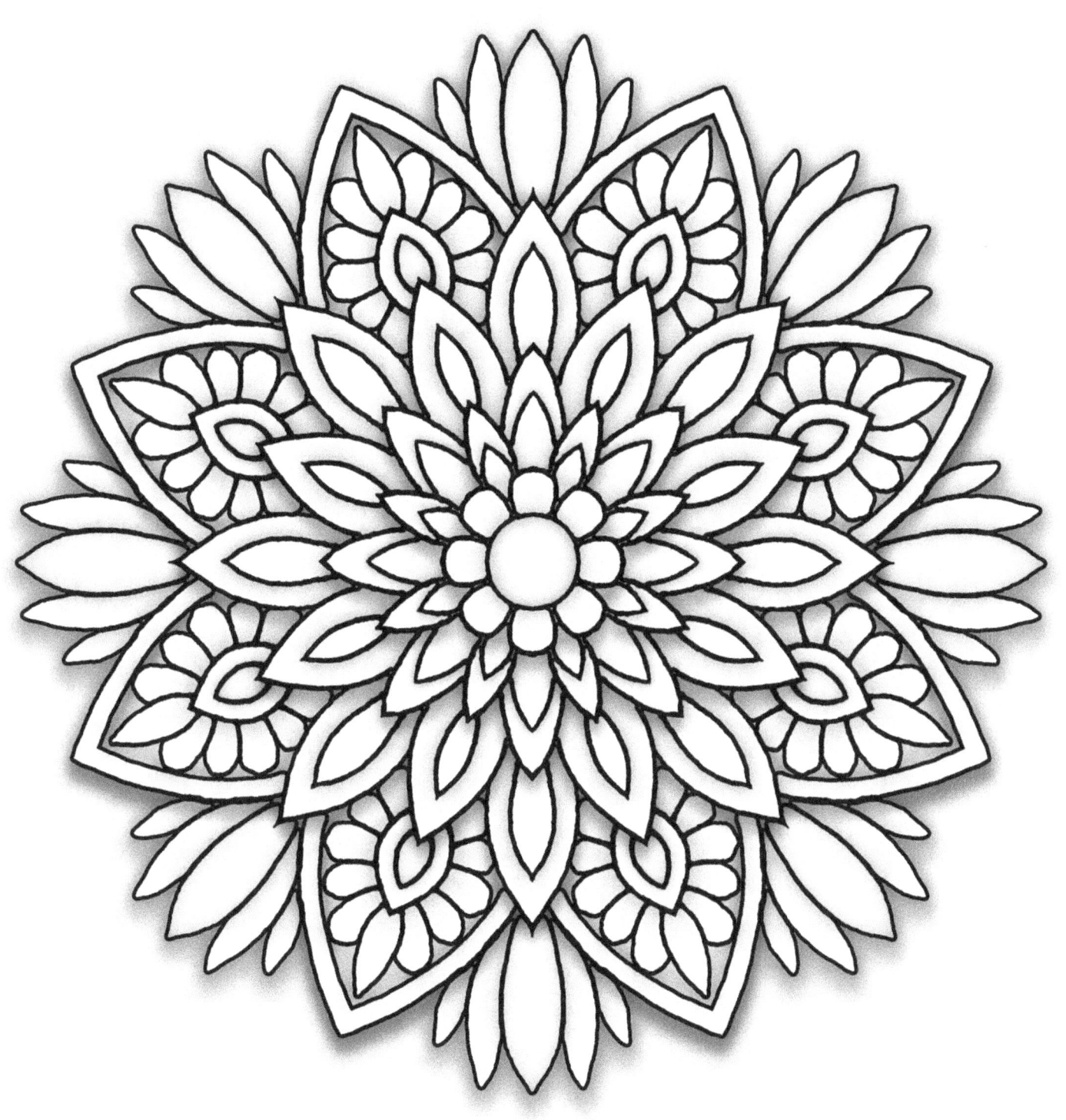

Floating 3d Mandalas 2

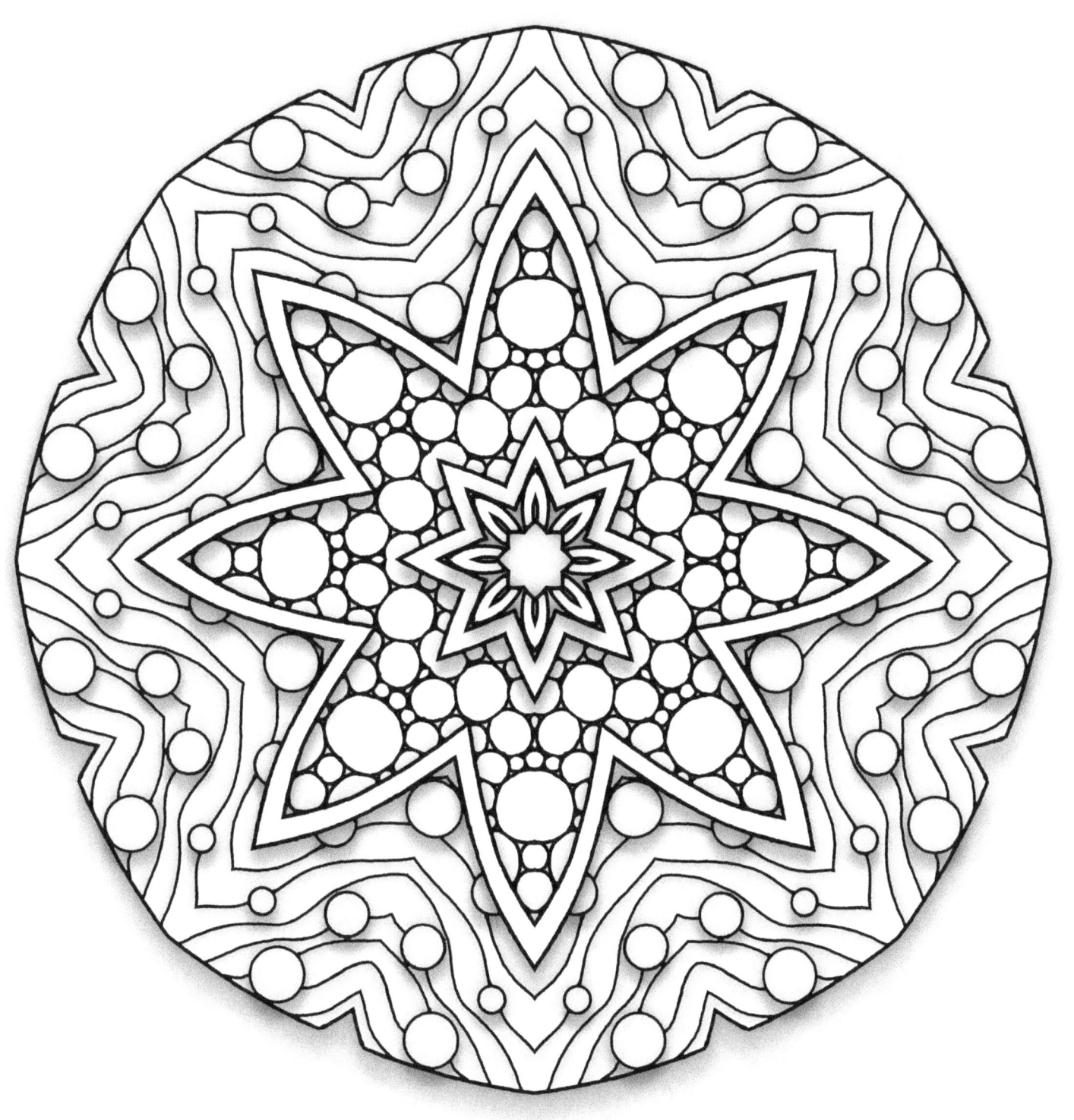

©2019 Tabitha Barnett

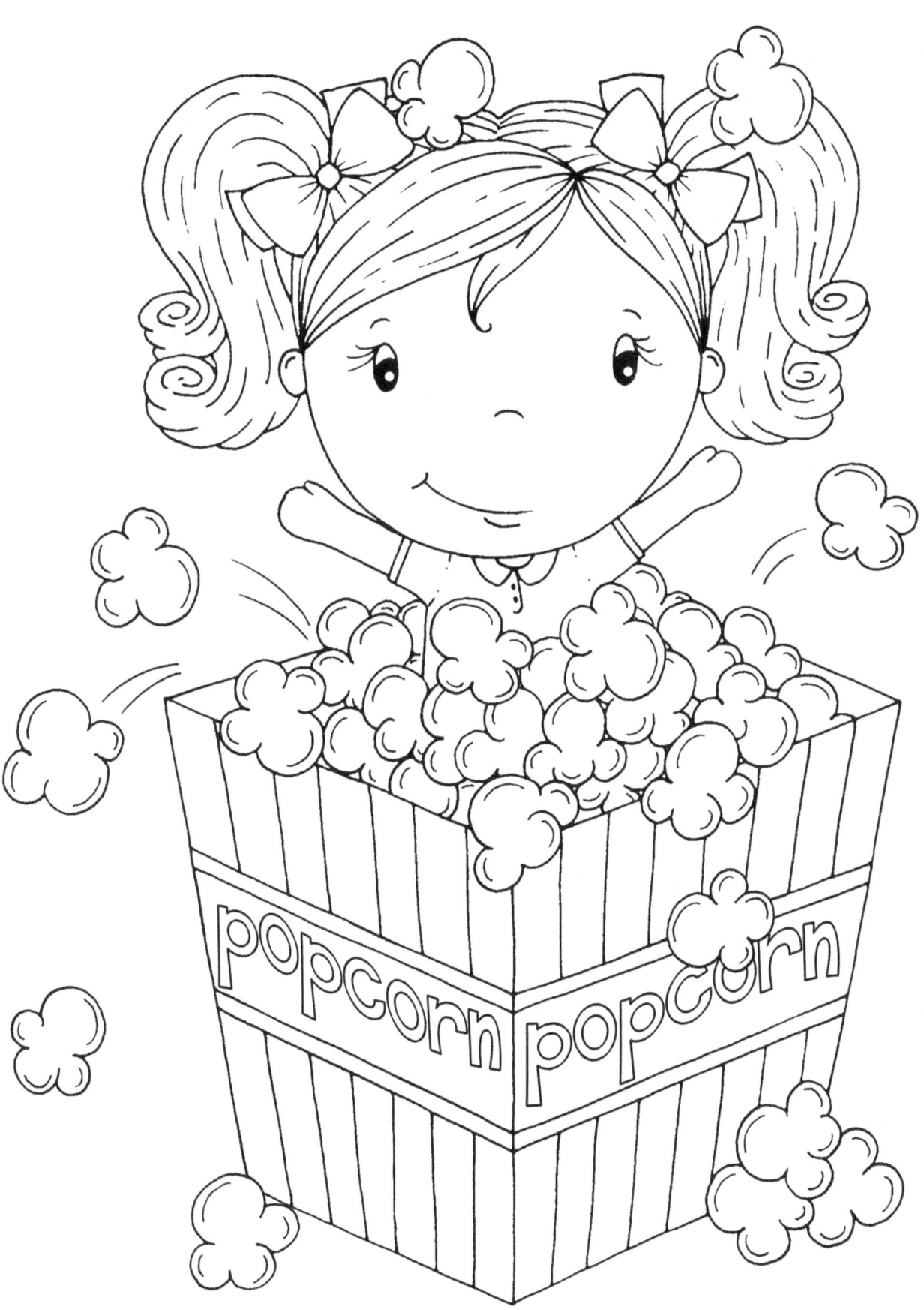

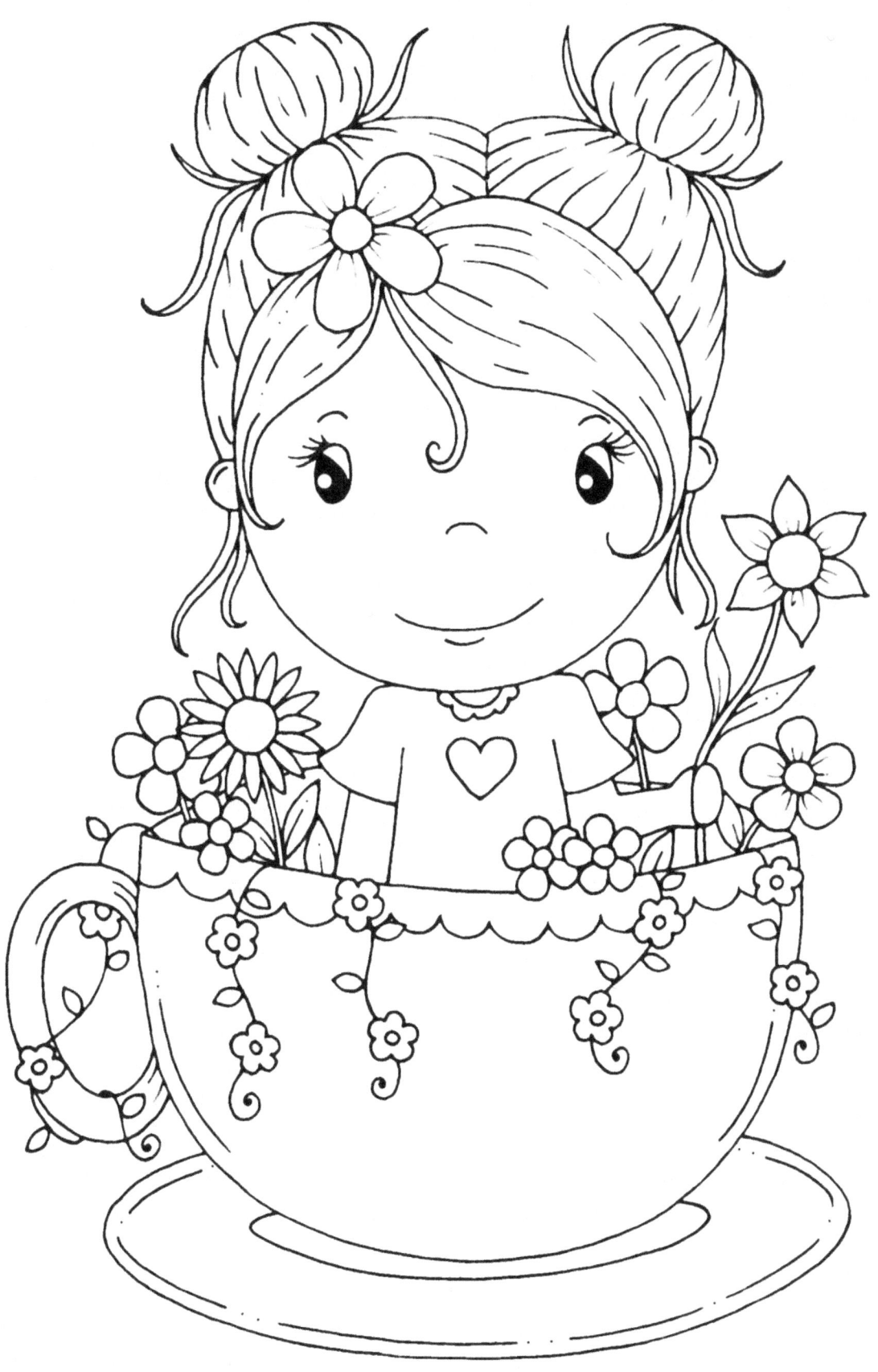

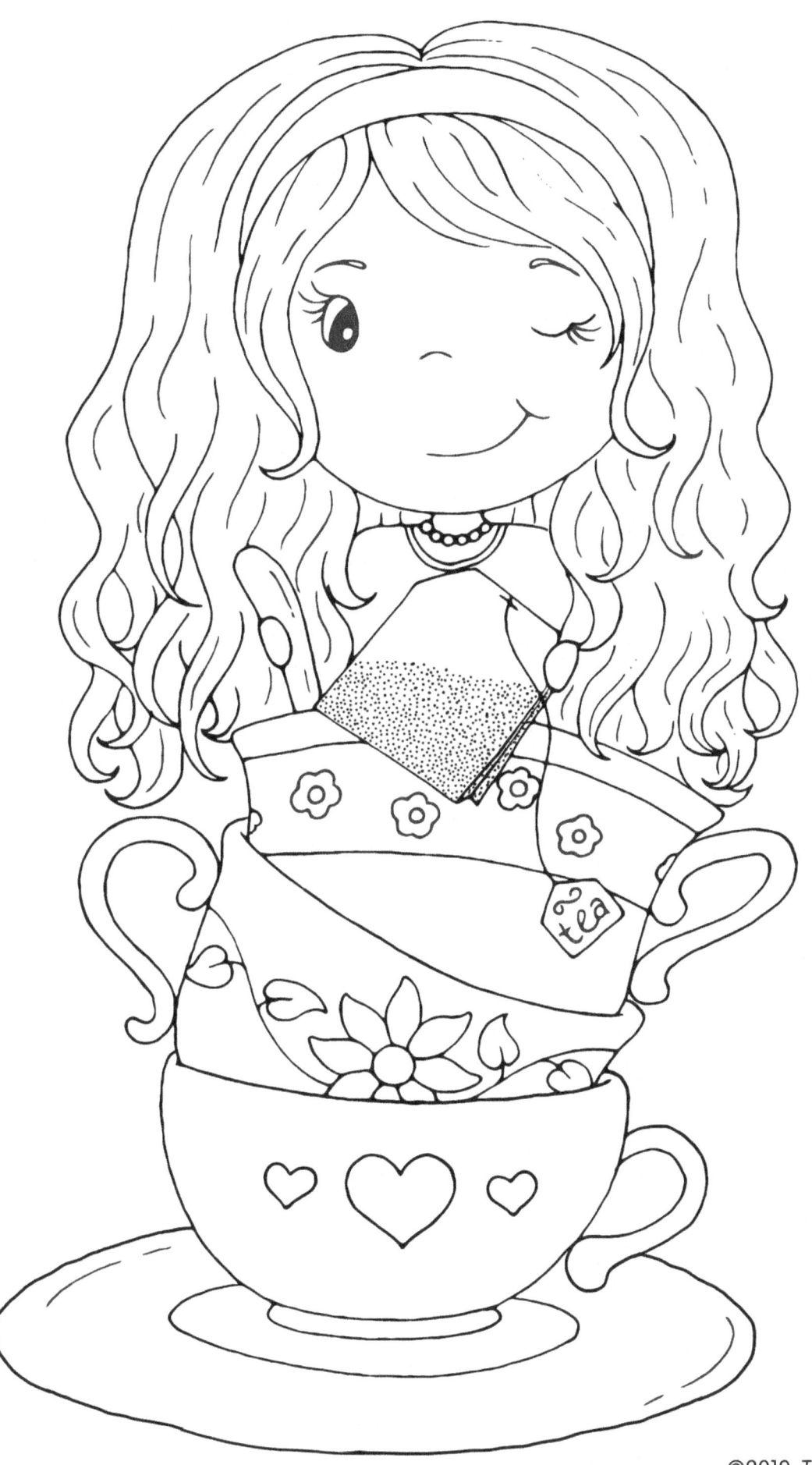

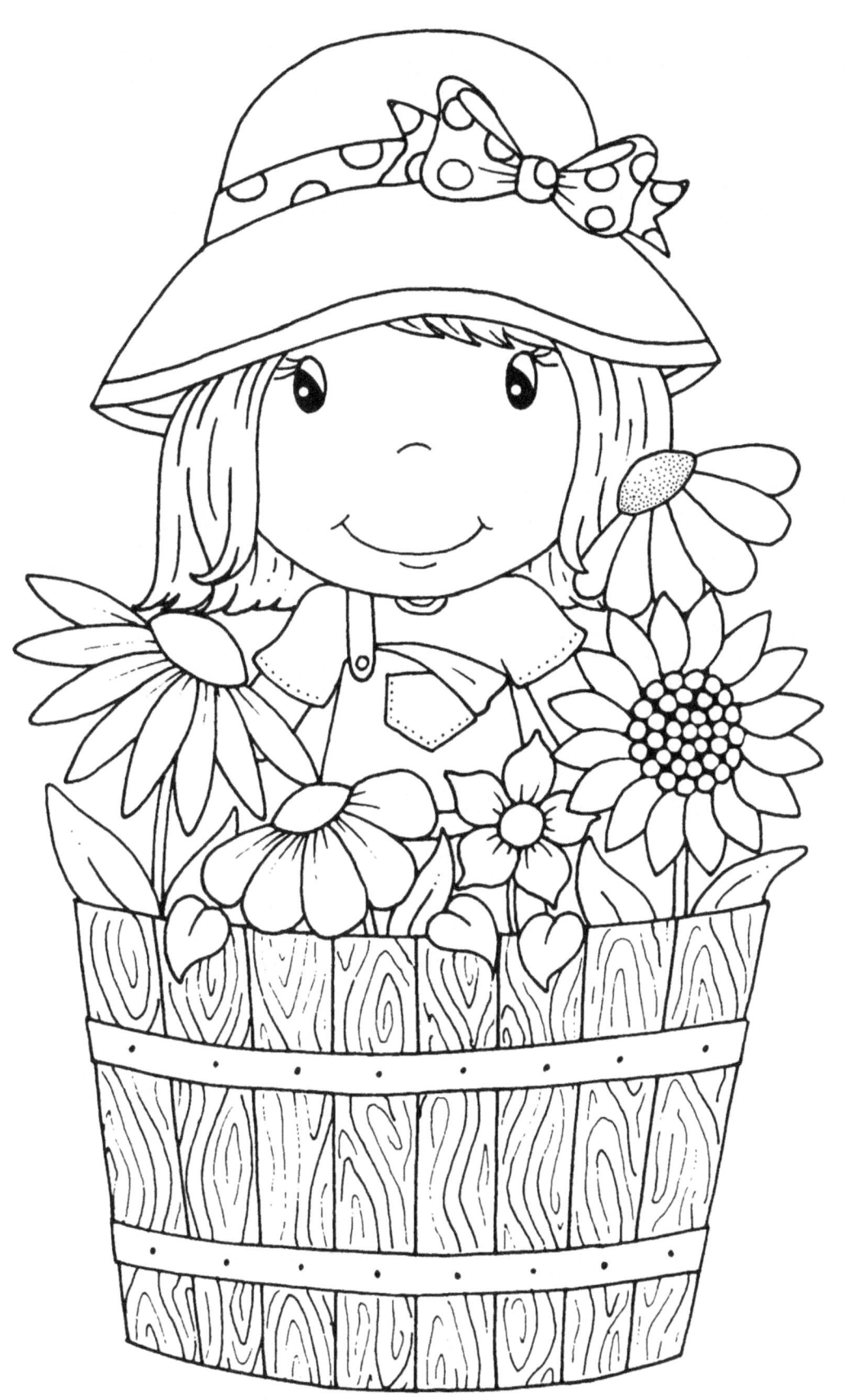

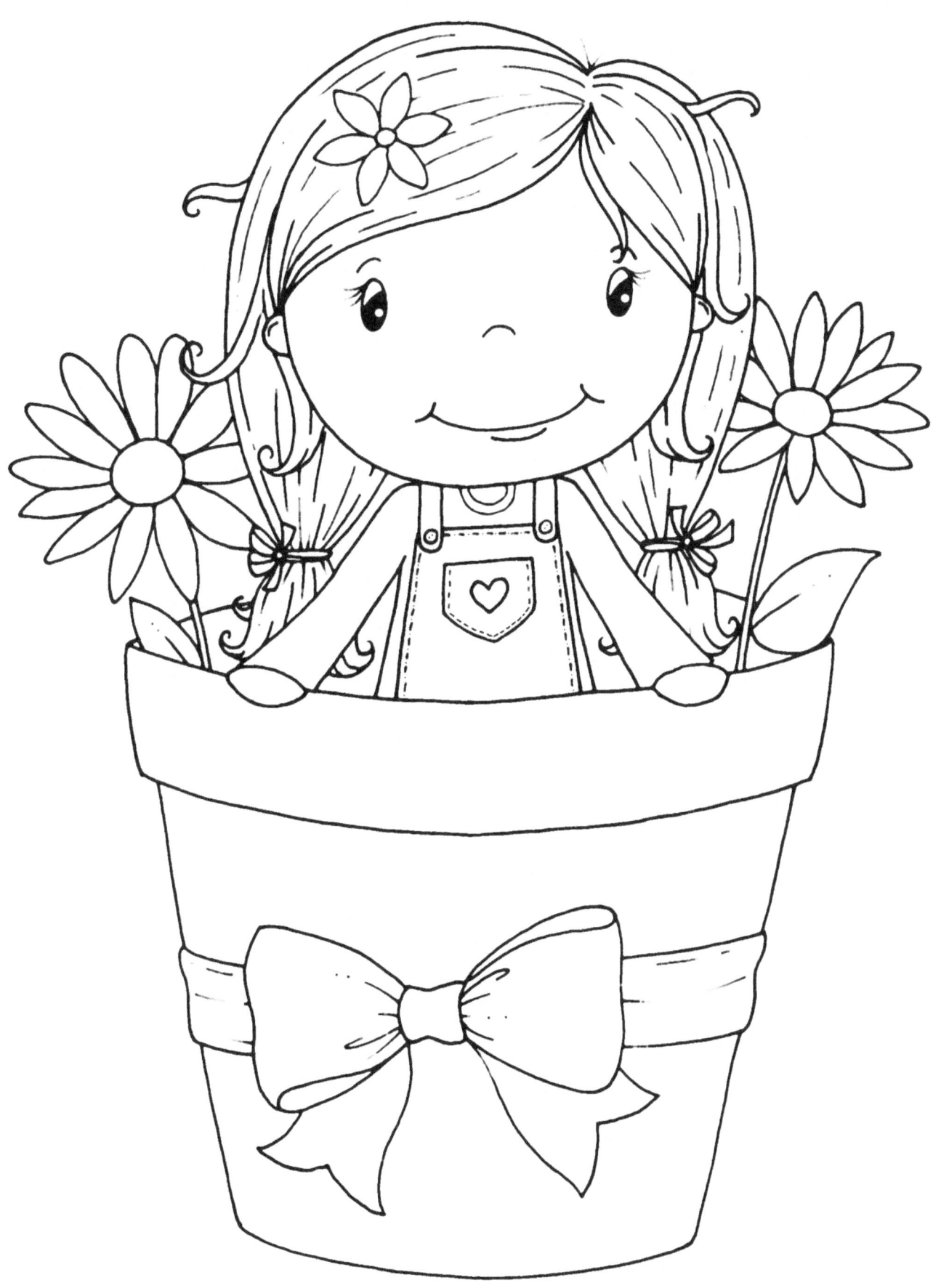

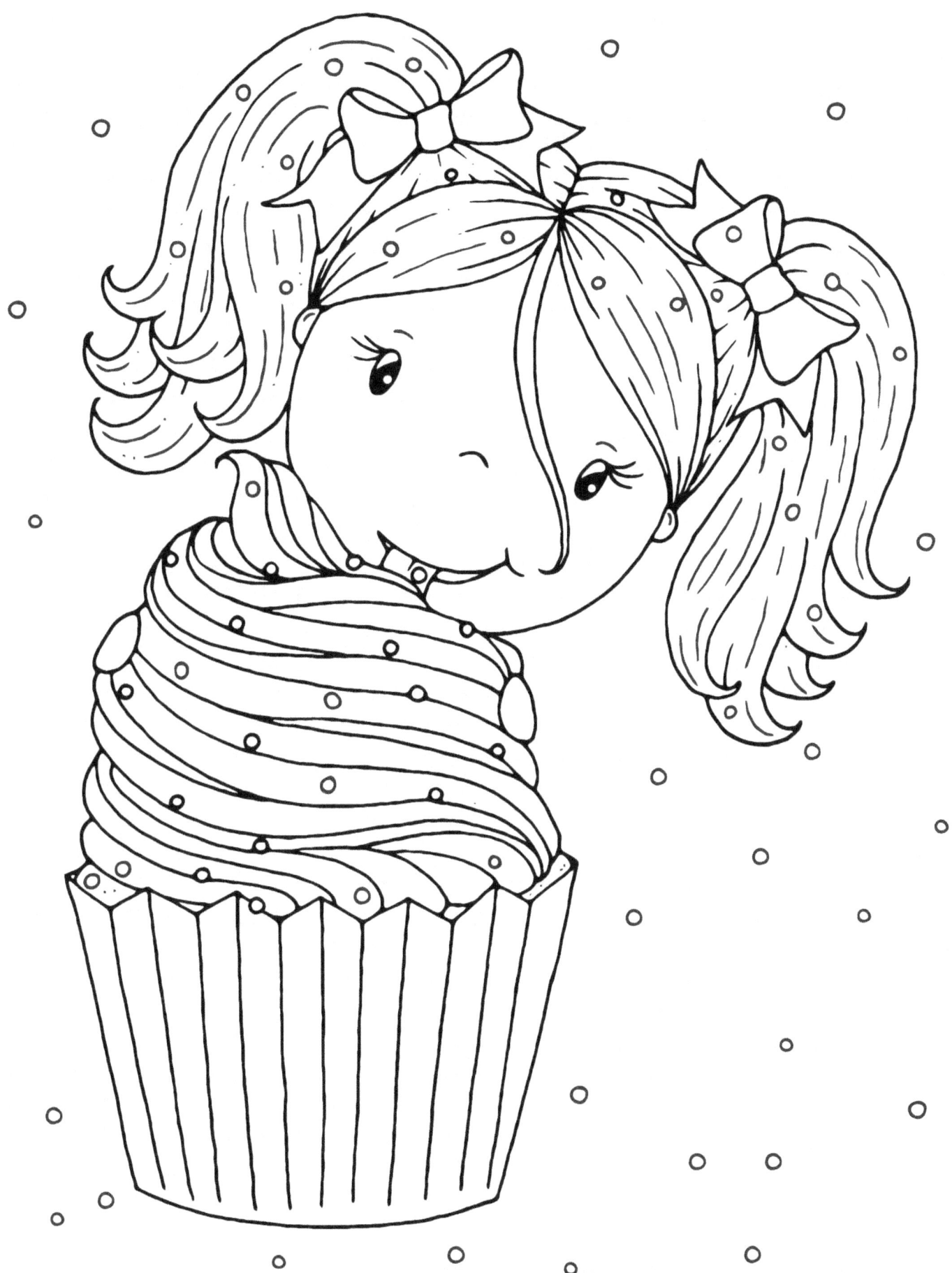

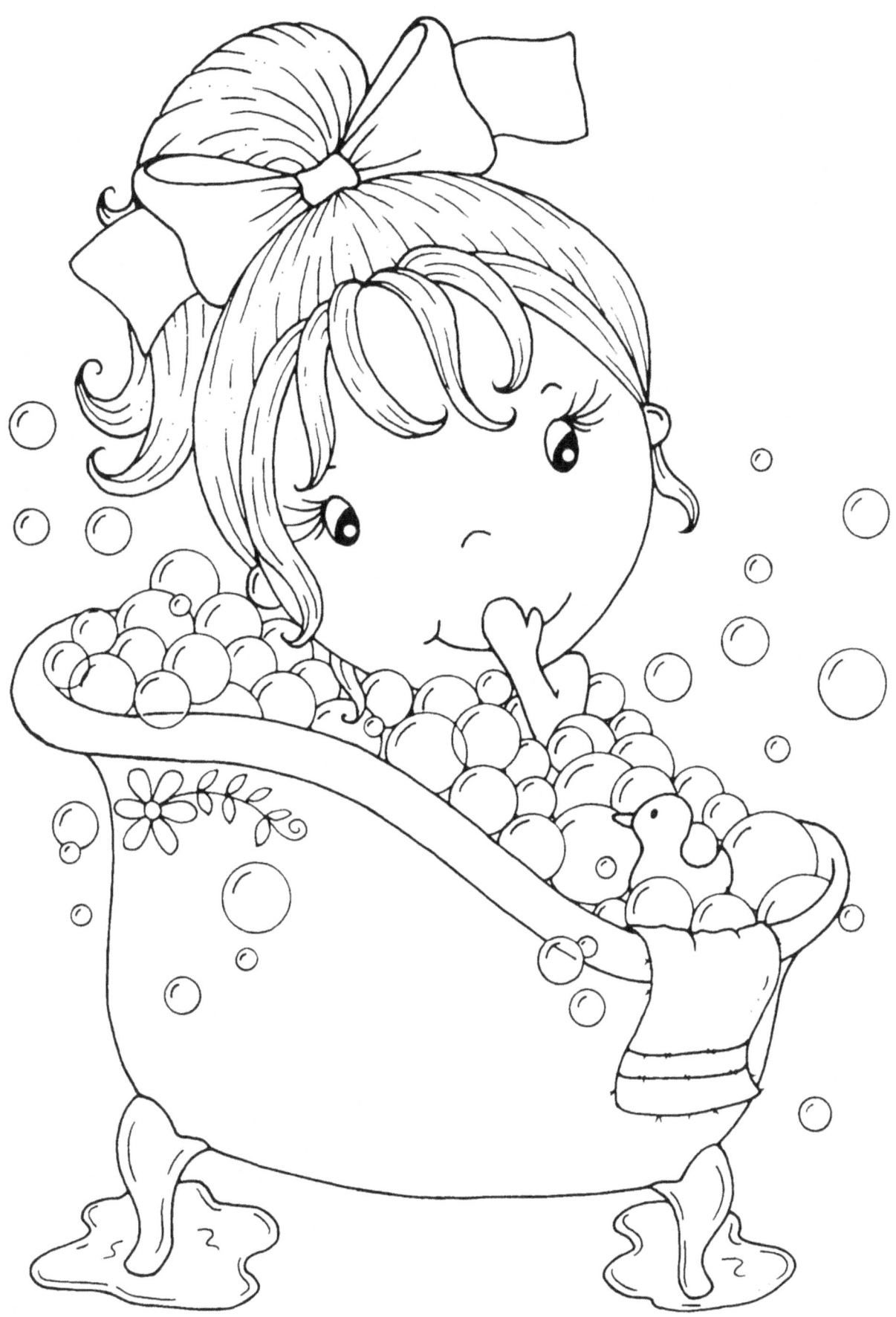

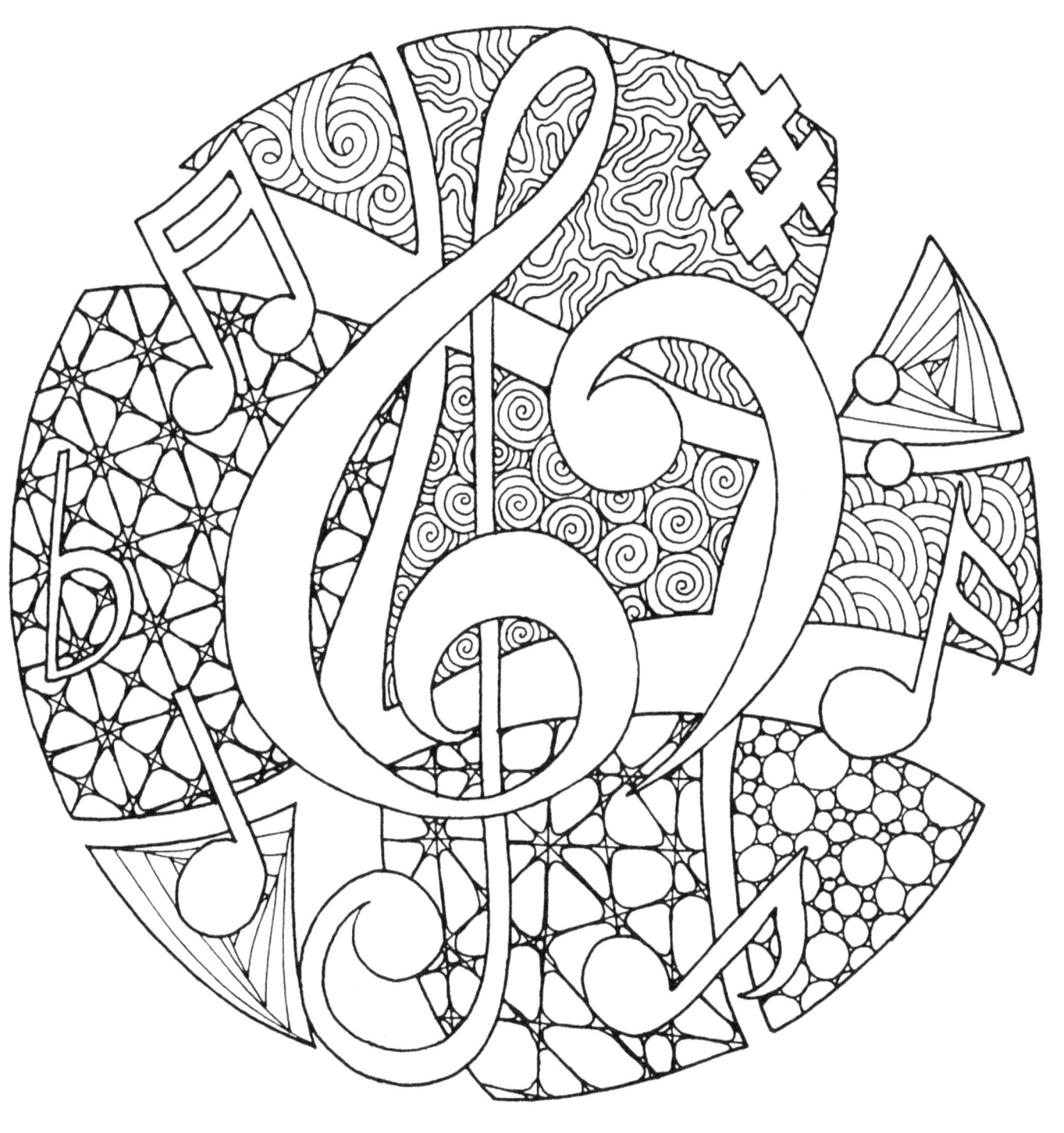

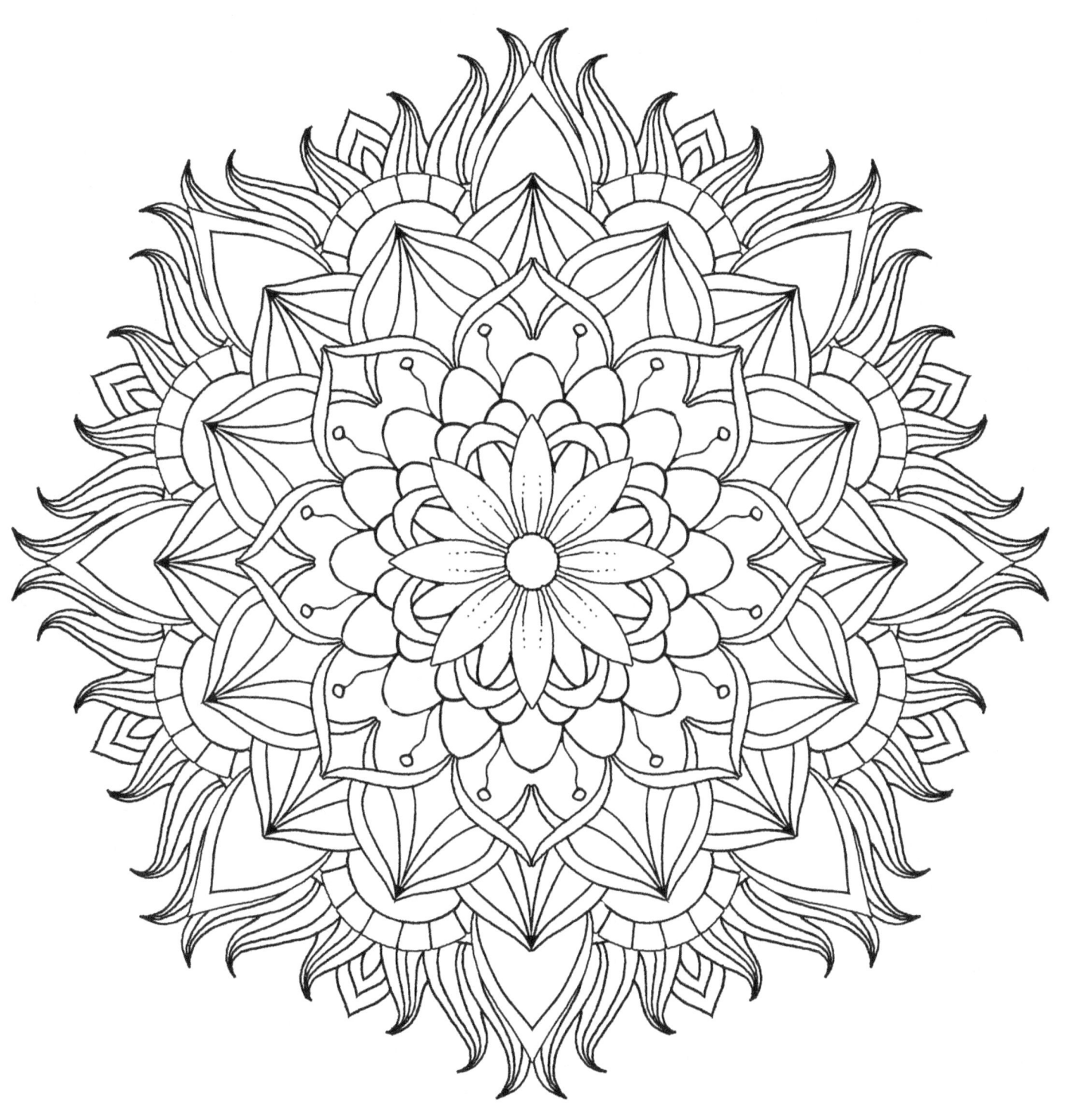

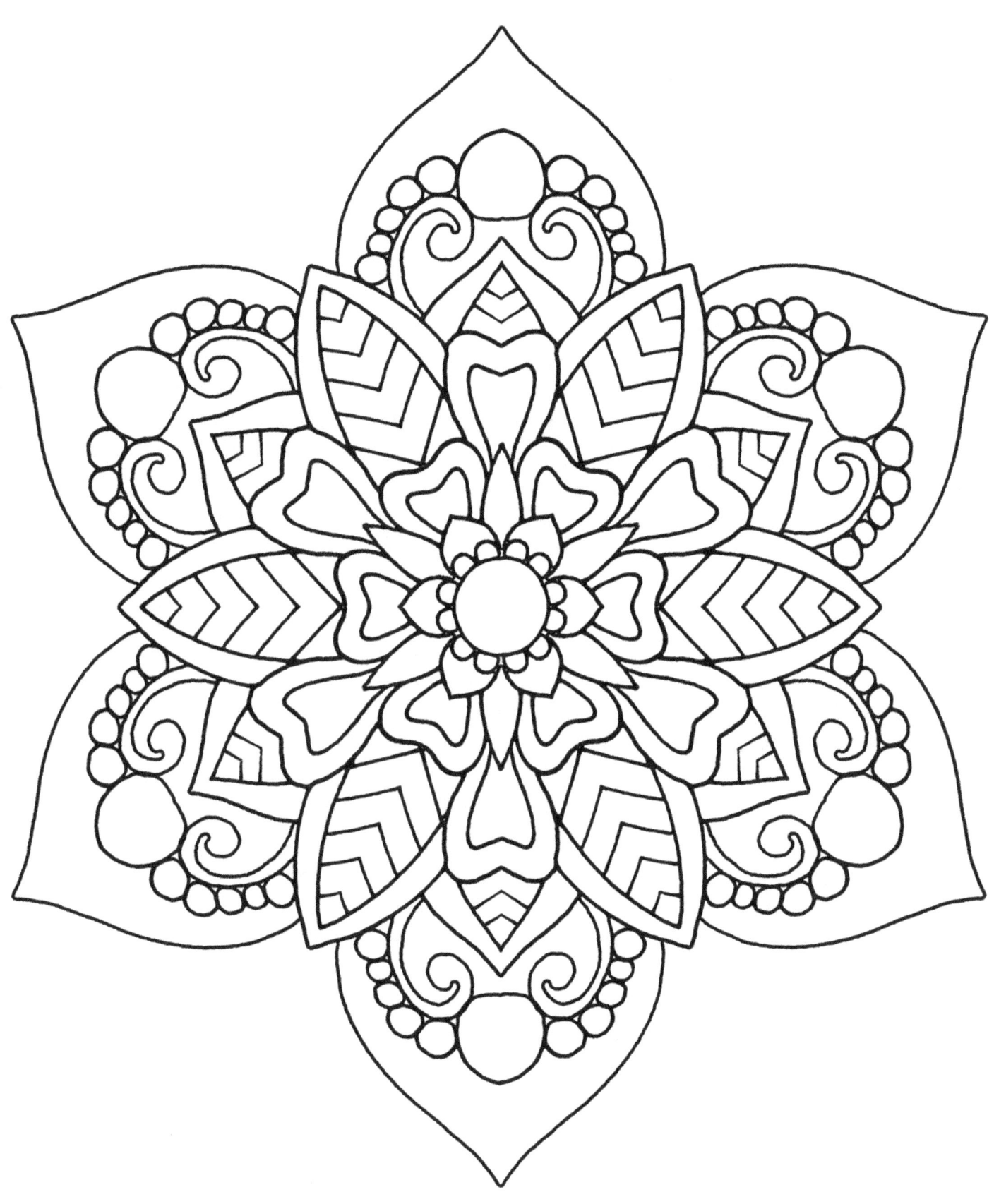

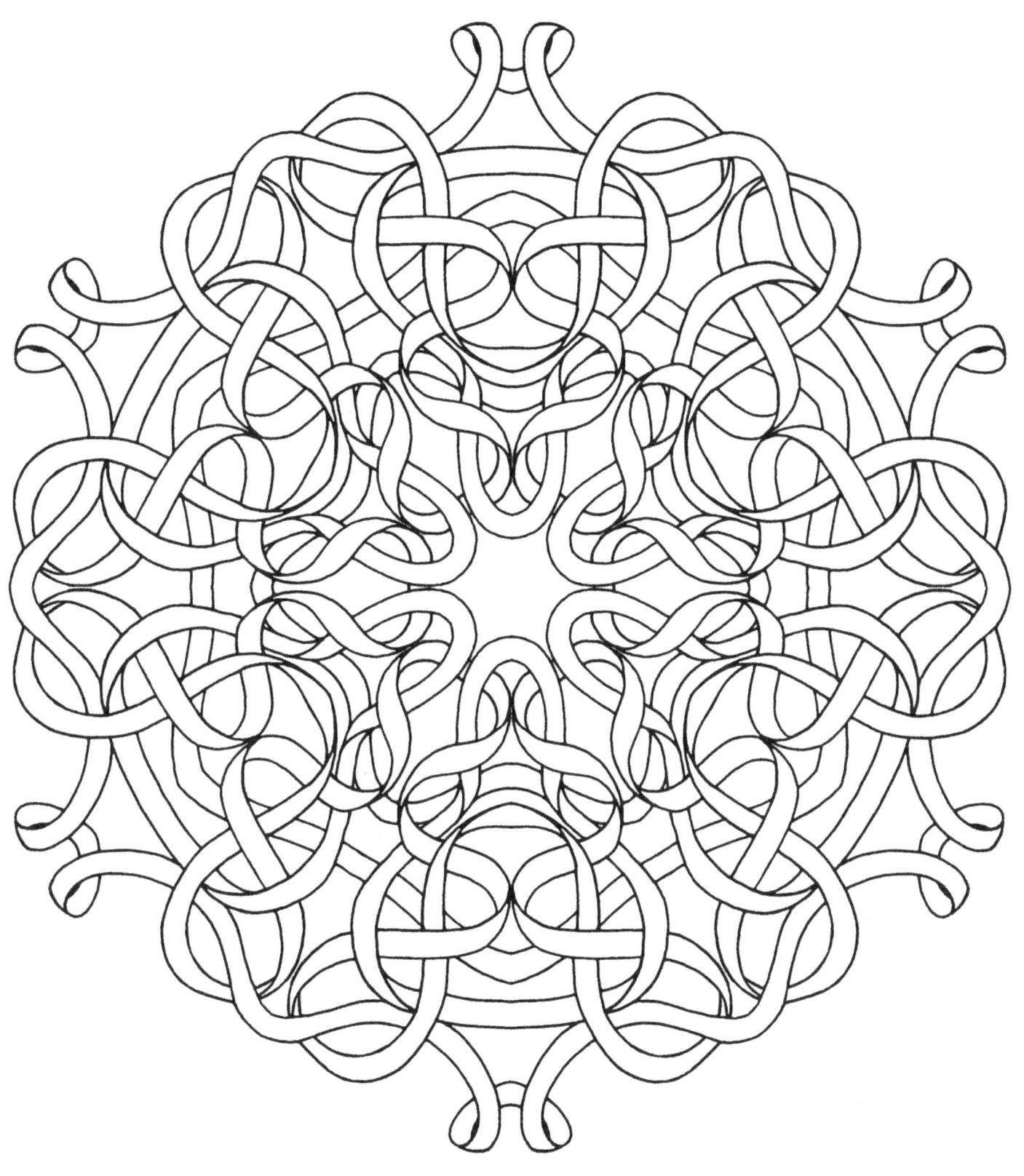

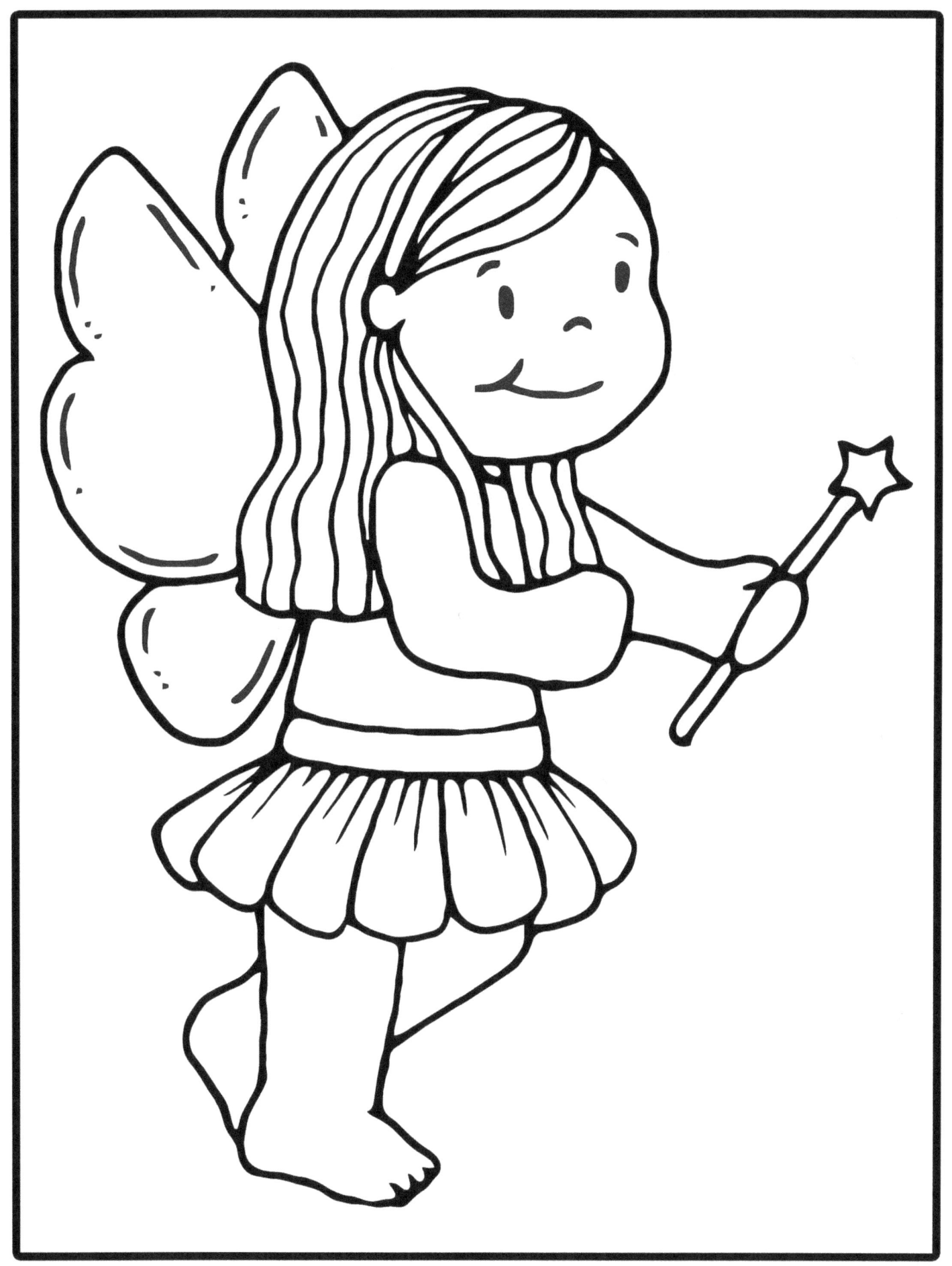

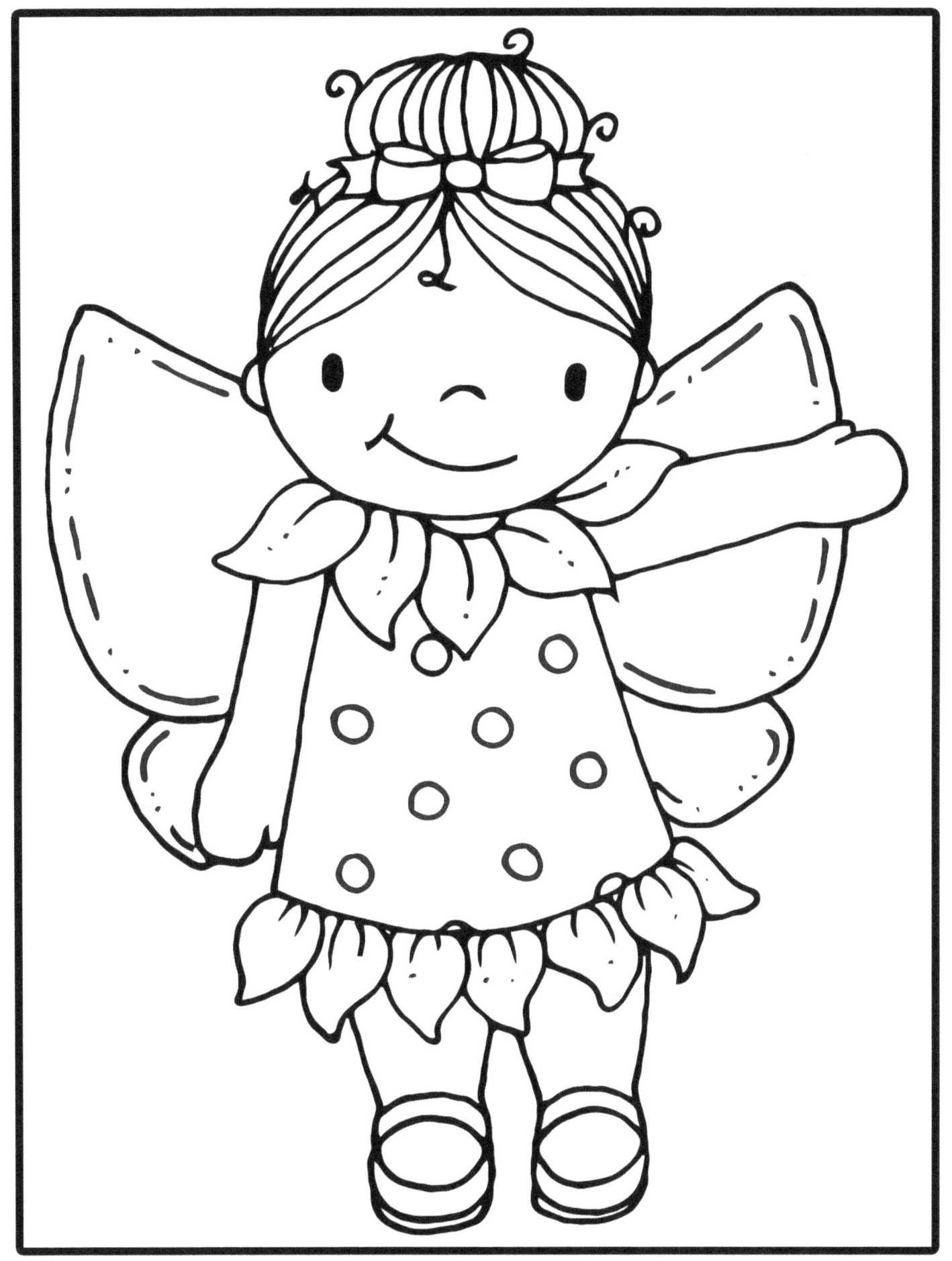

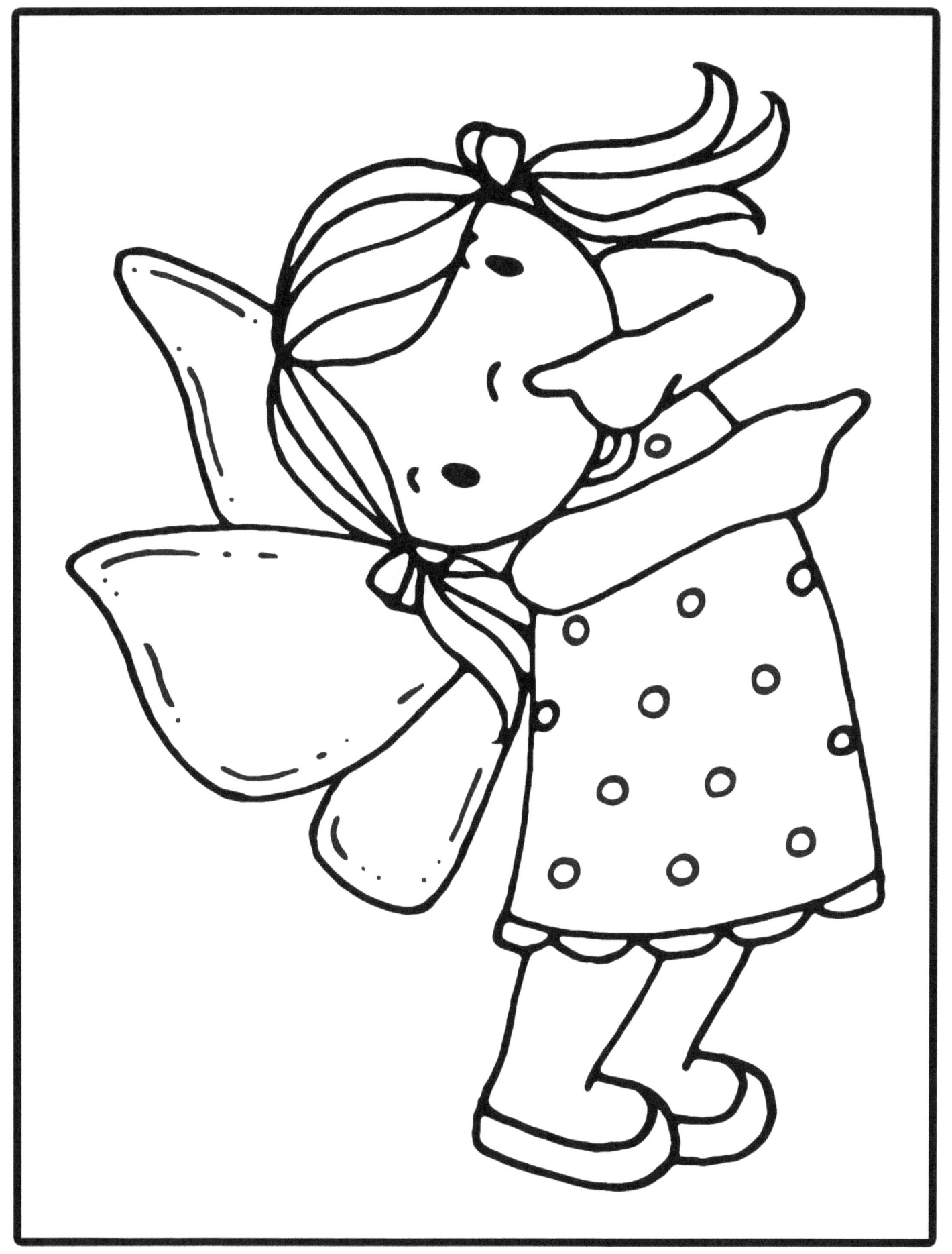

Meet the Fairies ©2019 Tabitha Barnett

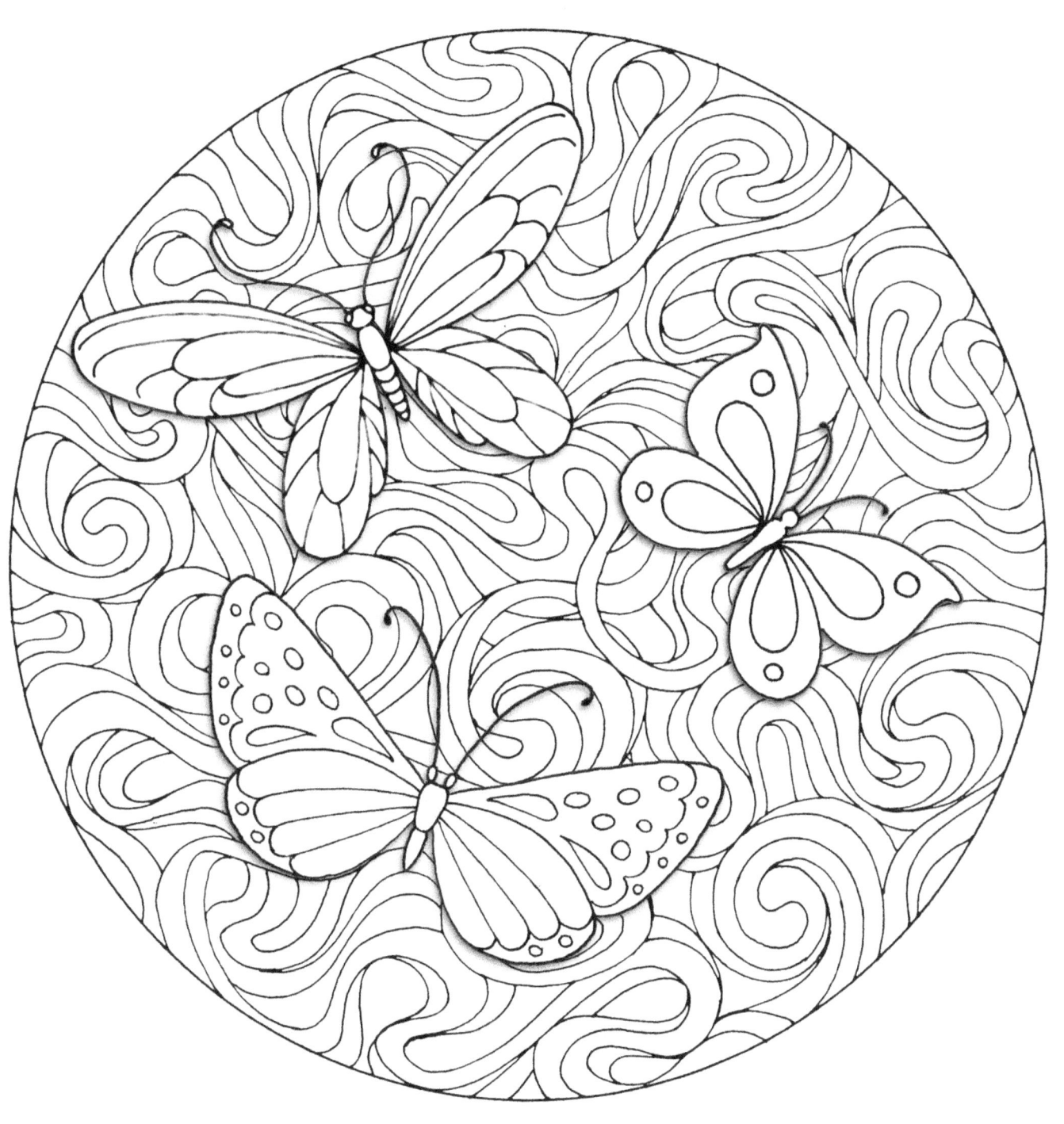

©2019 Tabitha Barnett

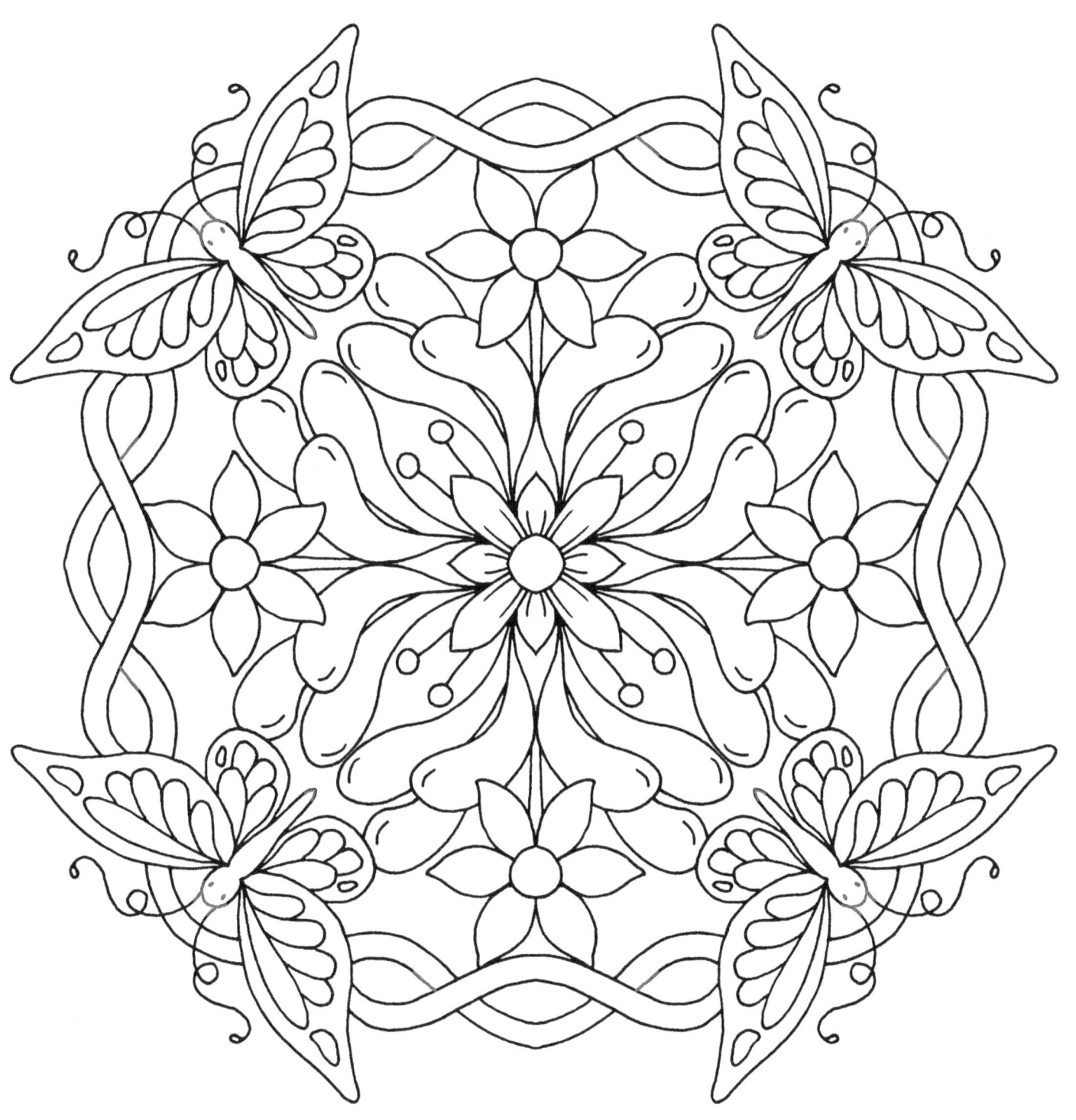

©2019 Tabitha Barnett

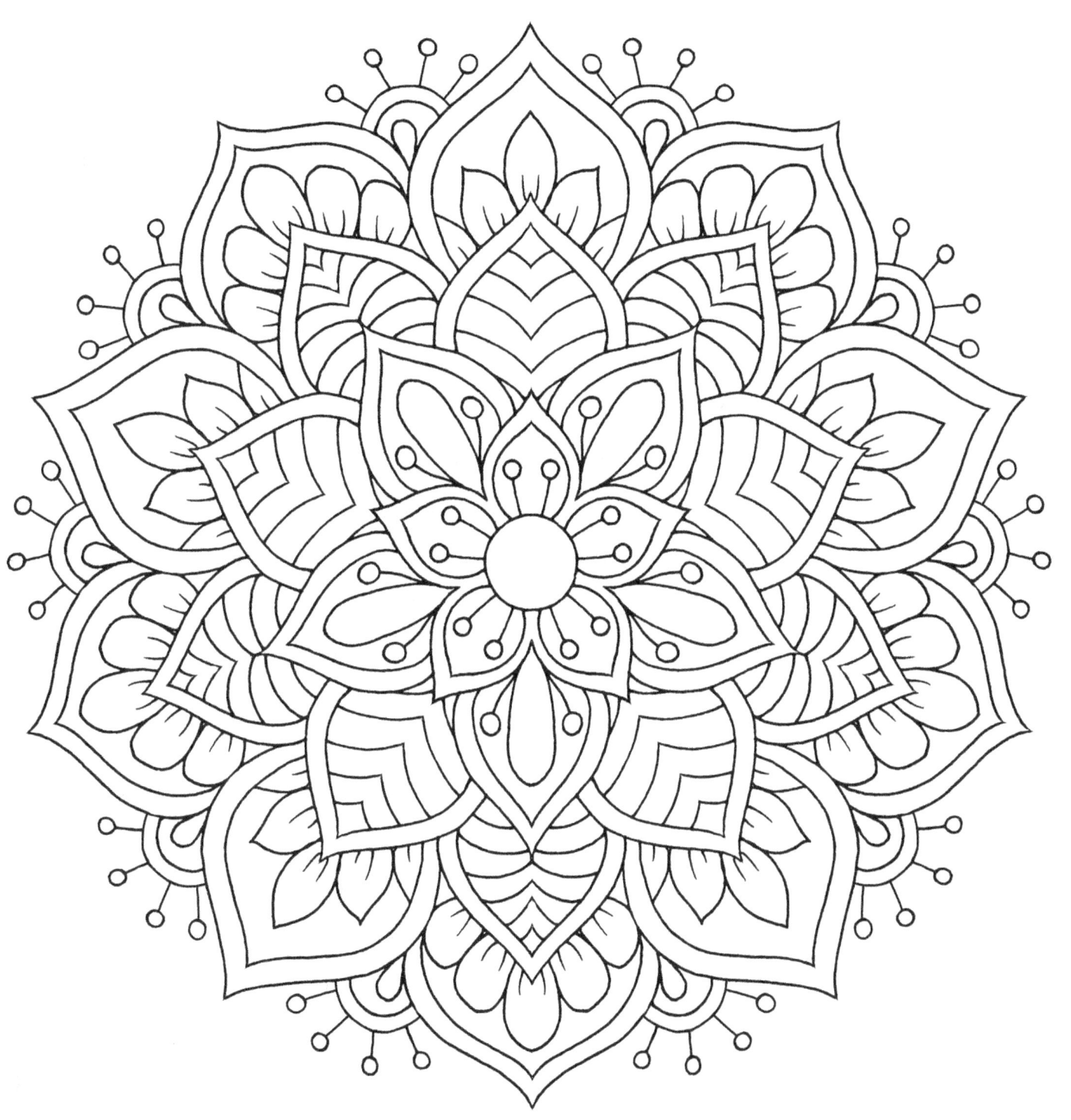

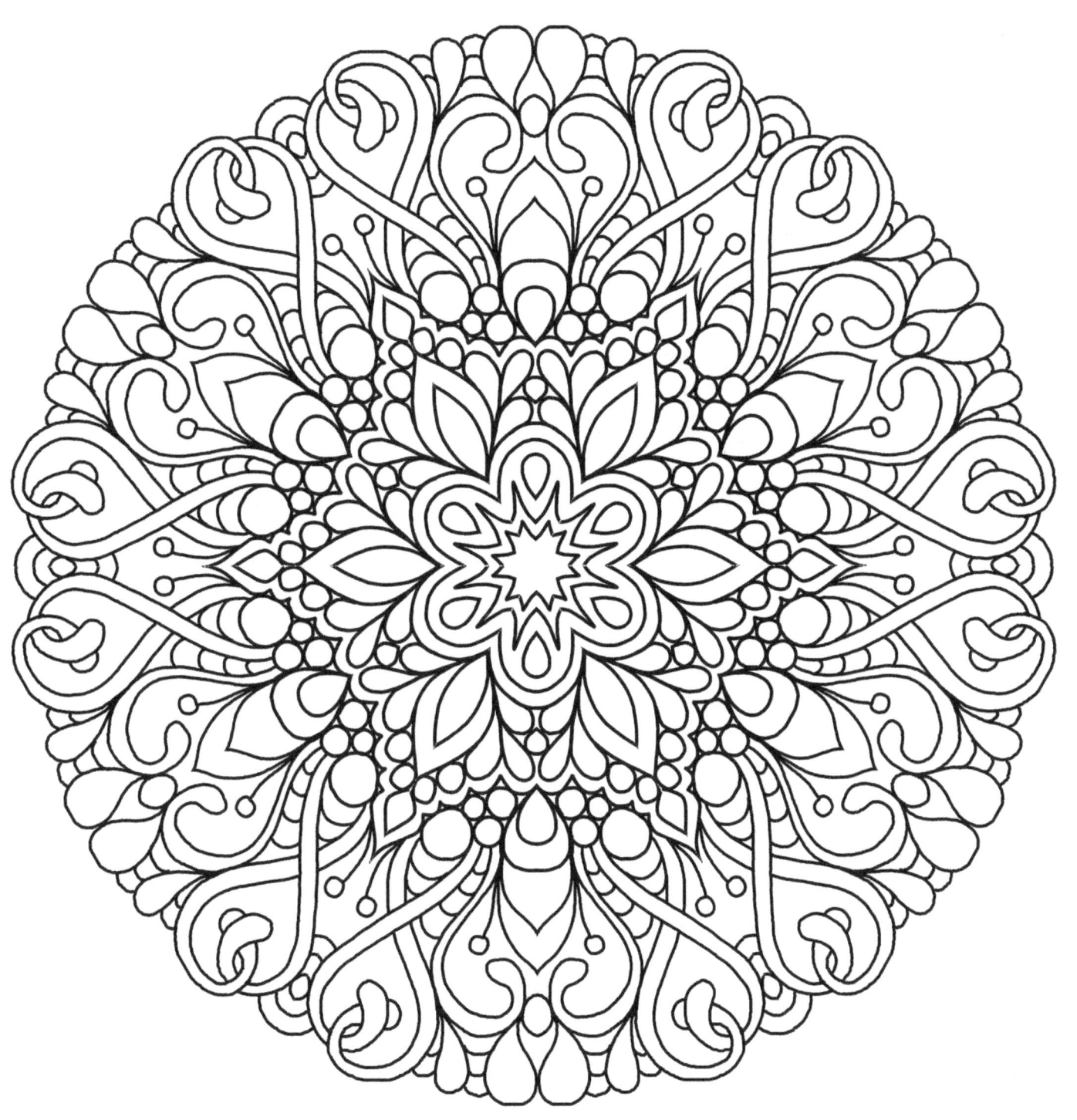
©2019 Tabitha Barnett

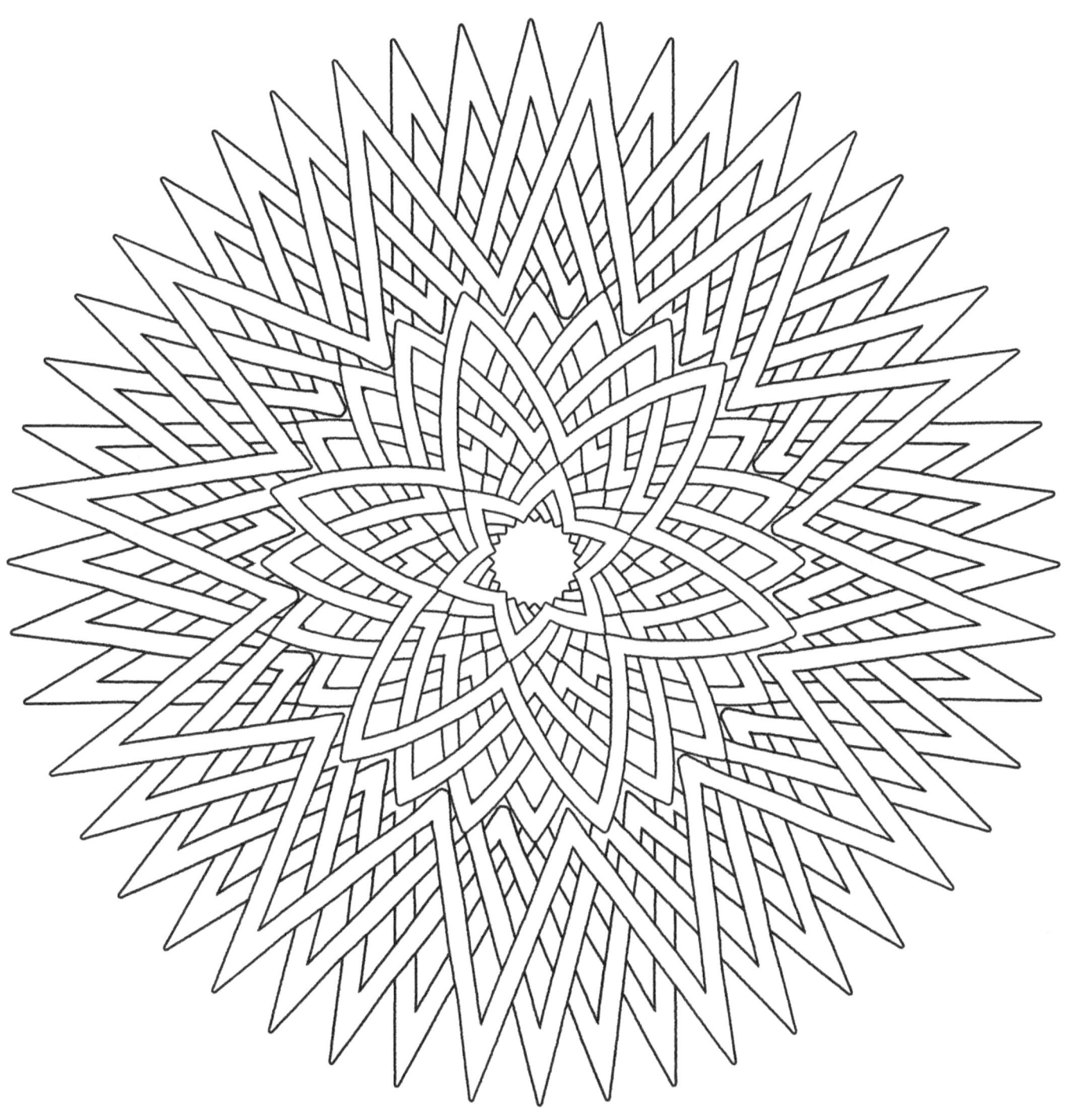

©2019 Tabitha Barnett

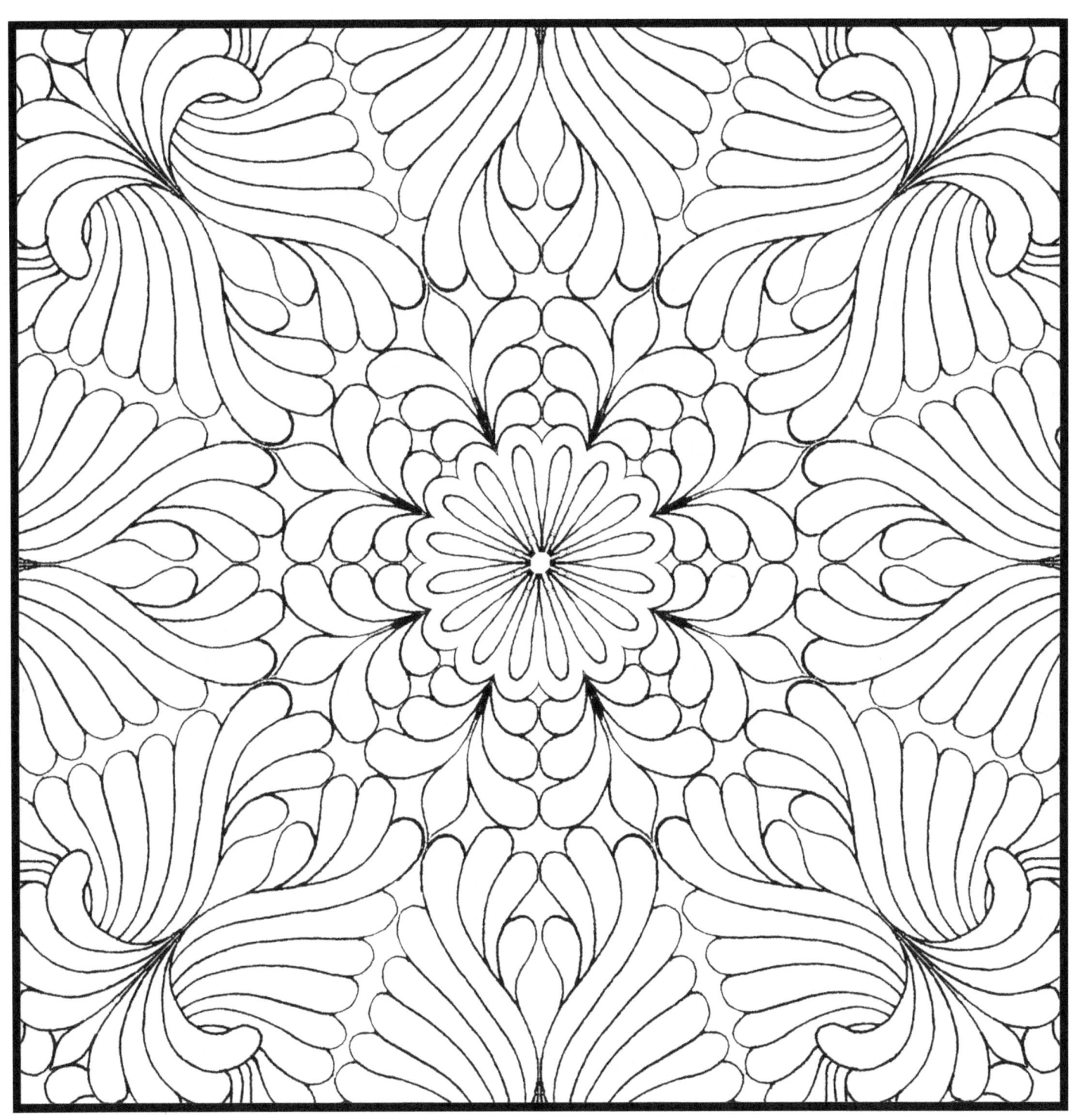

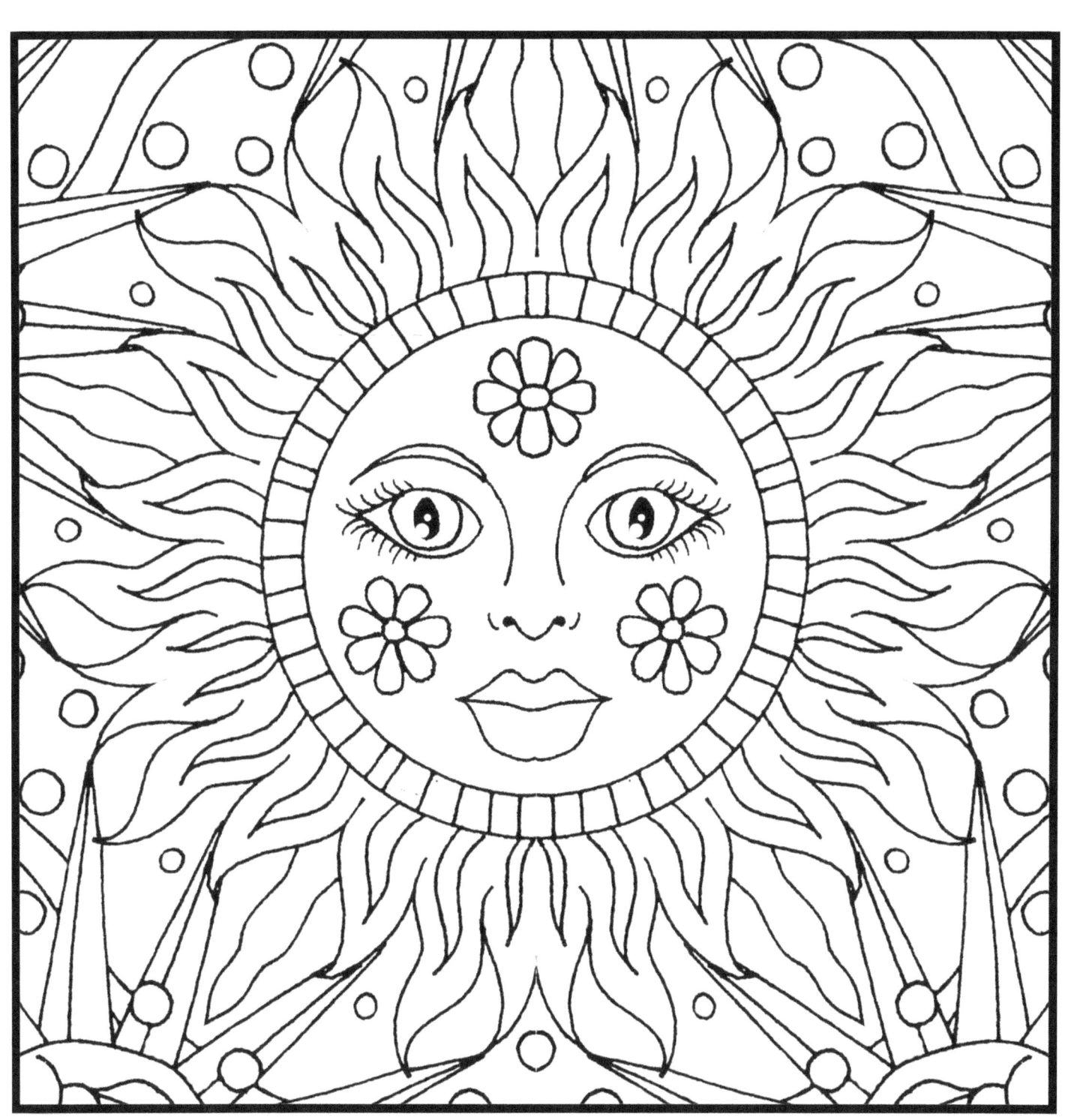

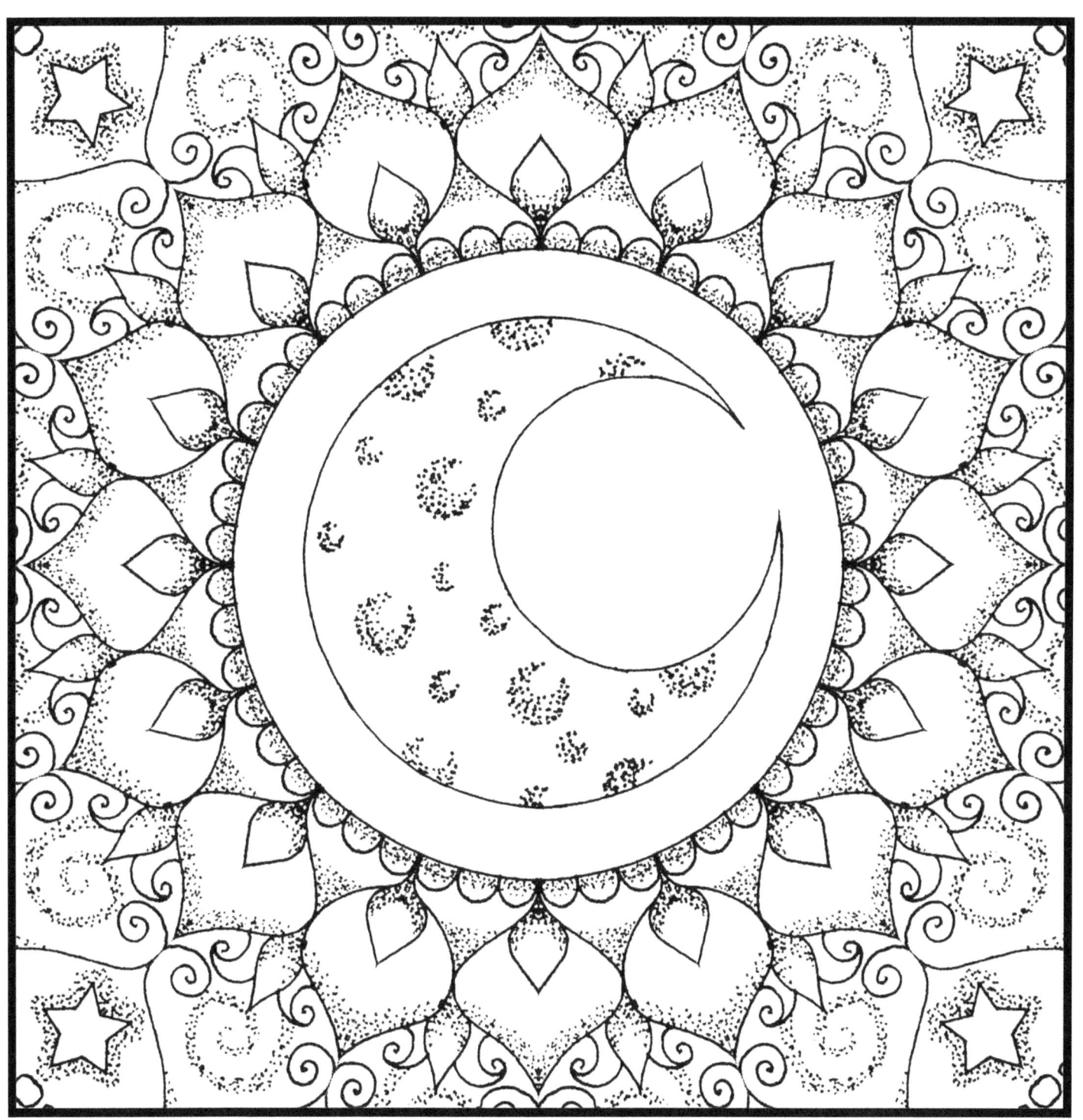

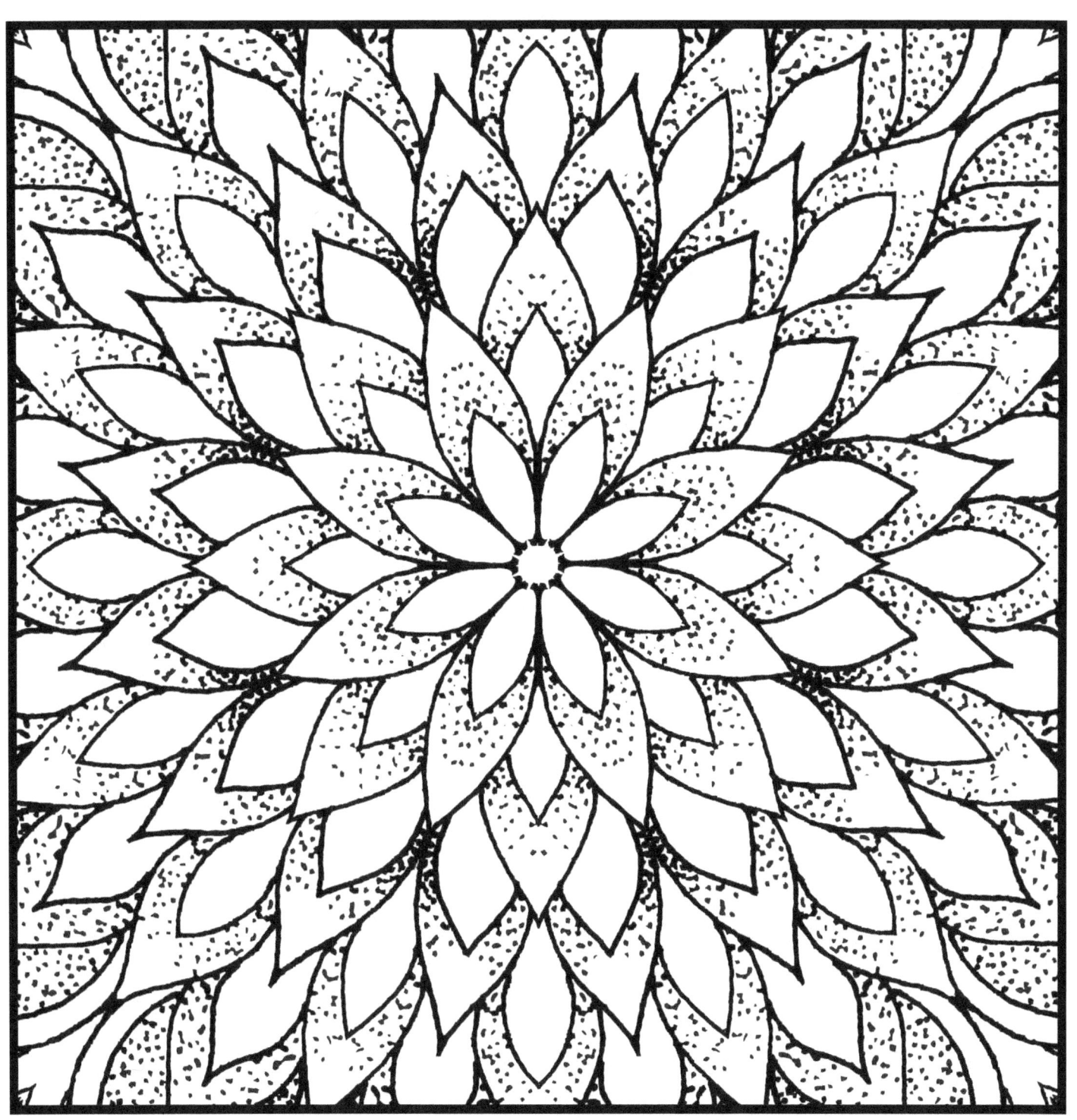

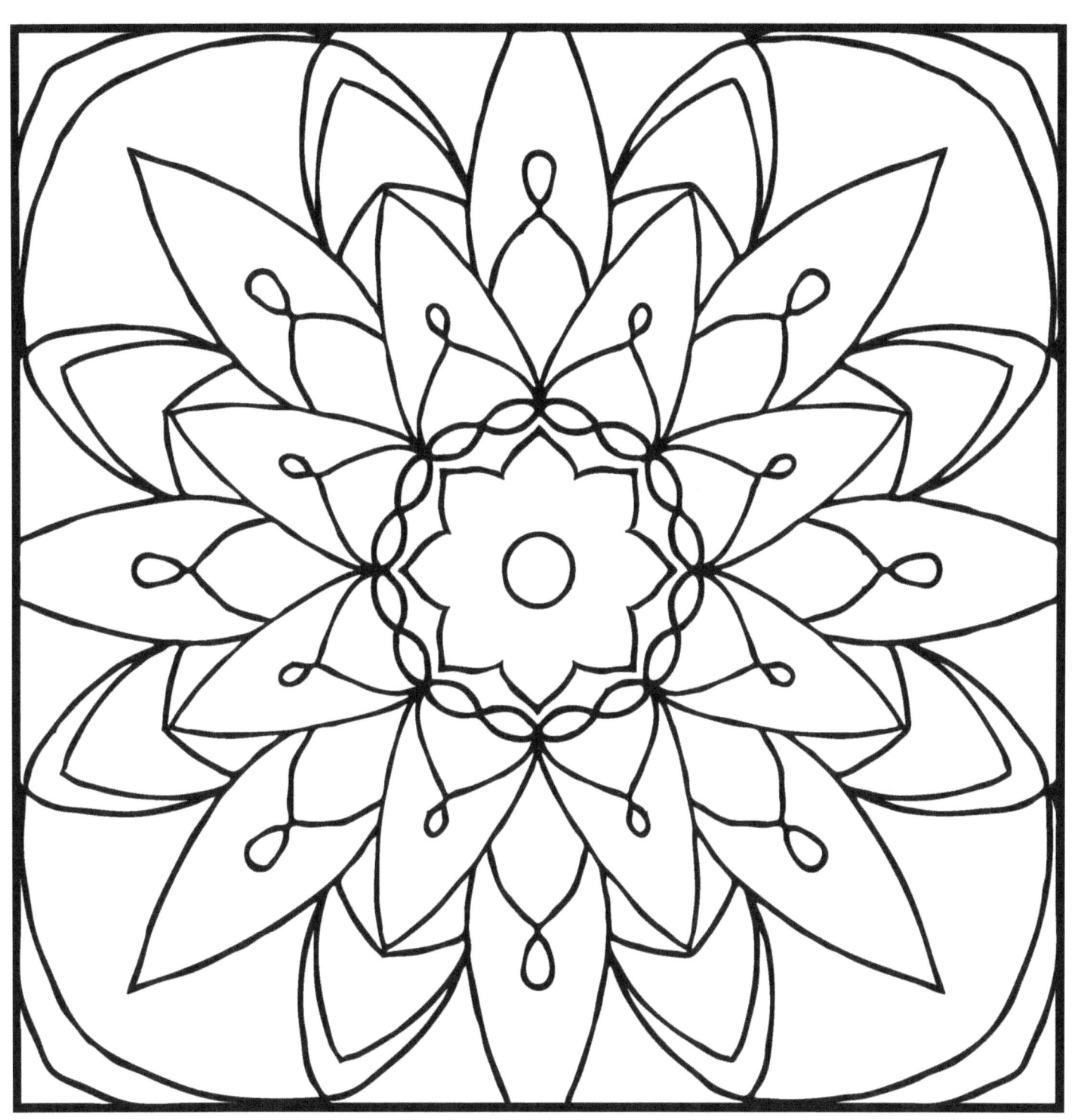

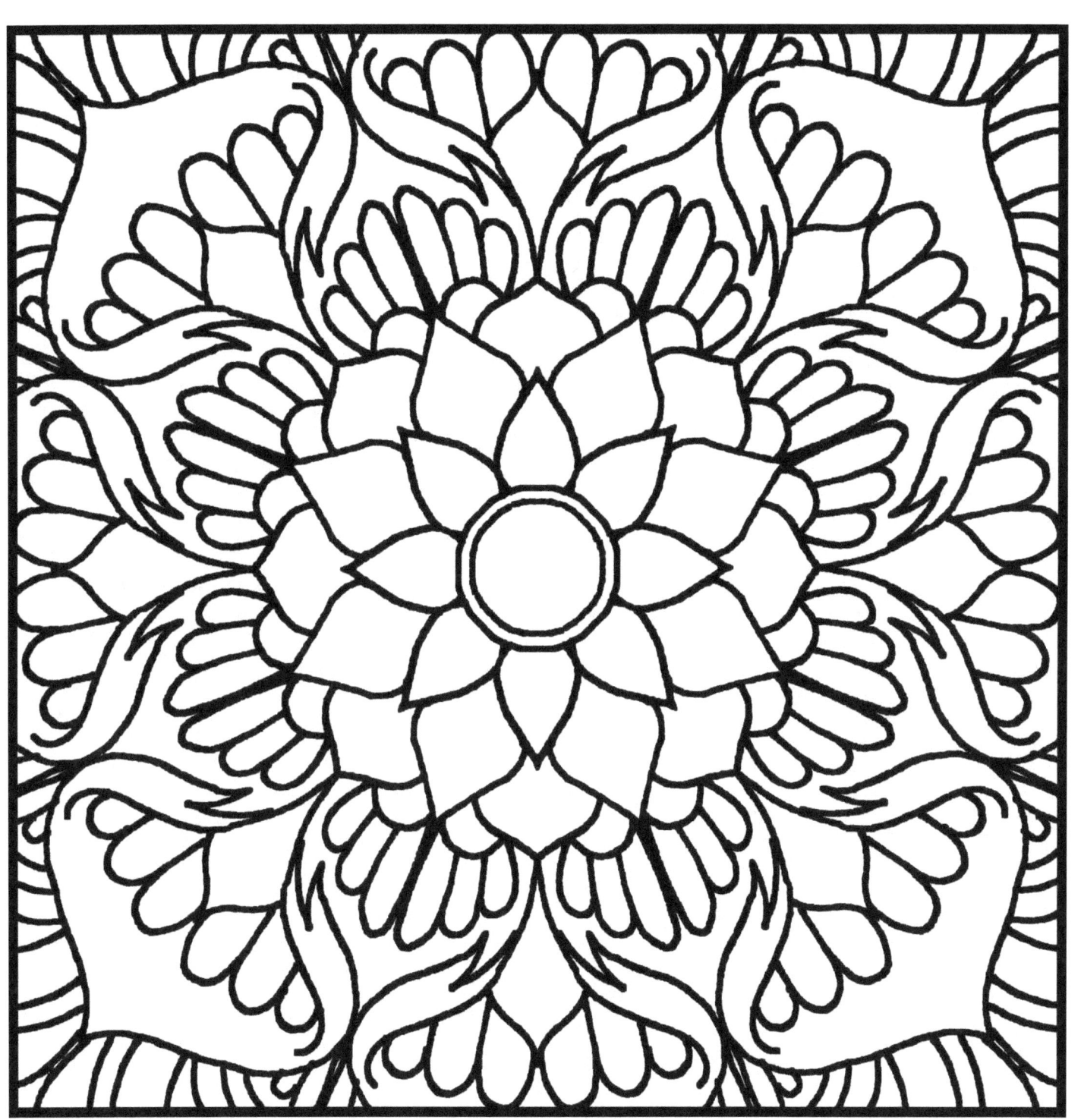

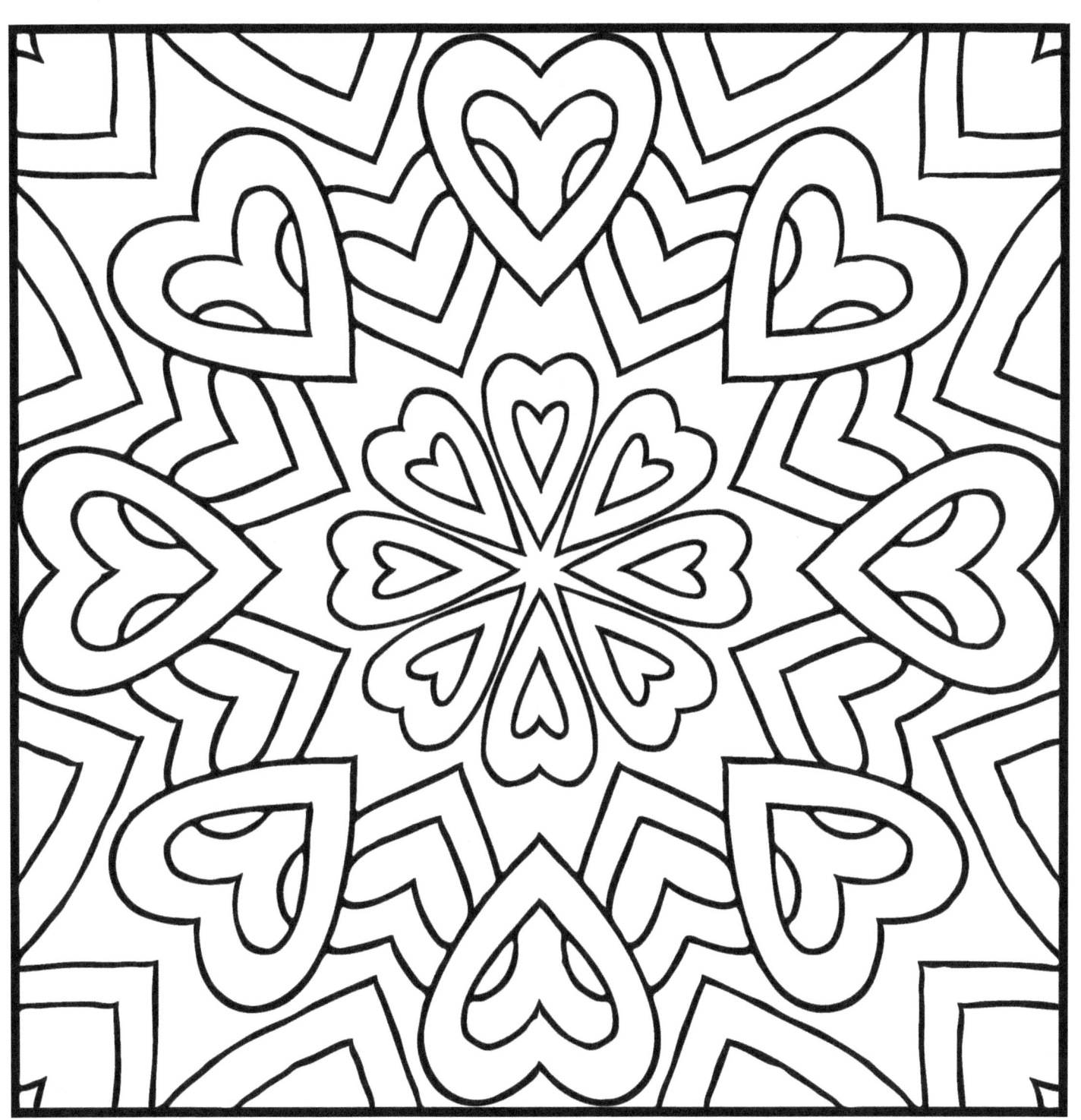

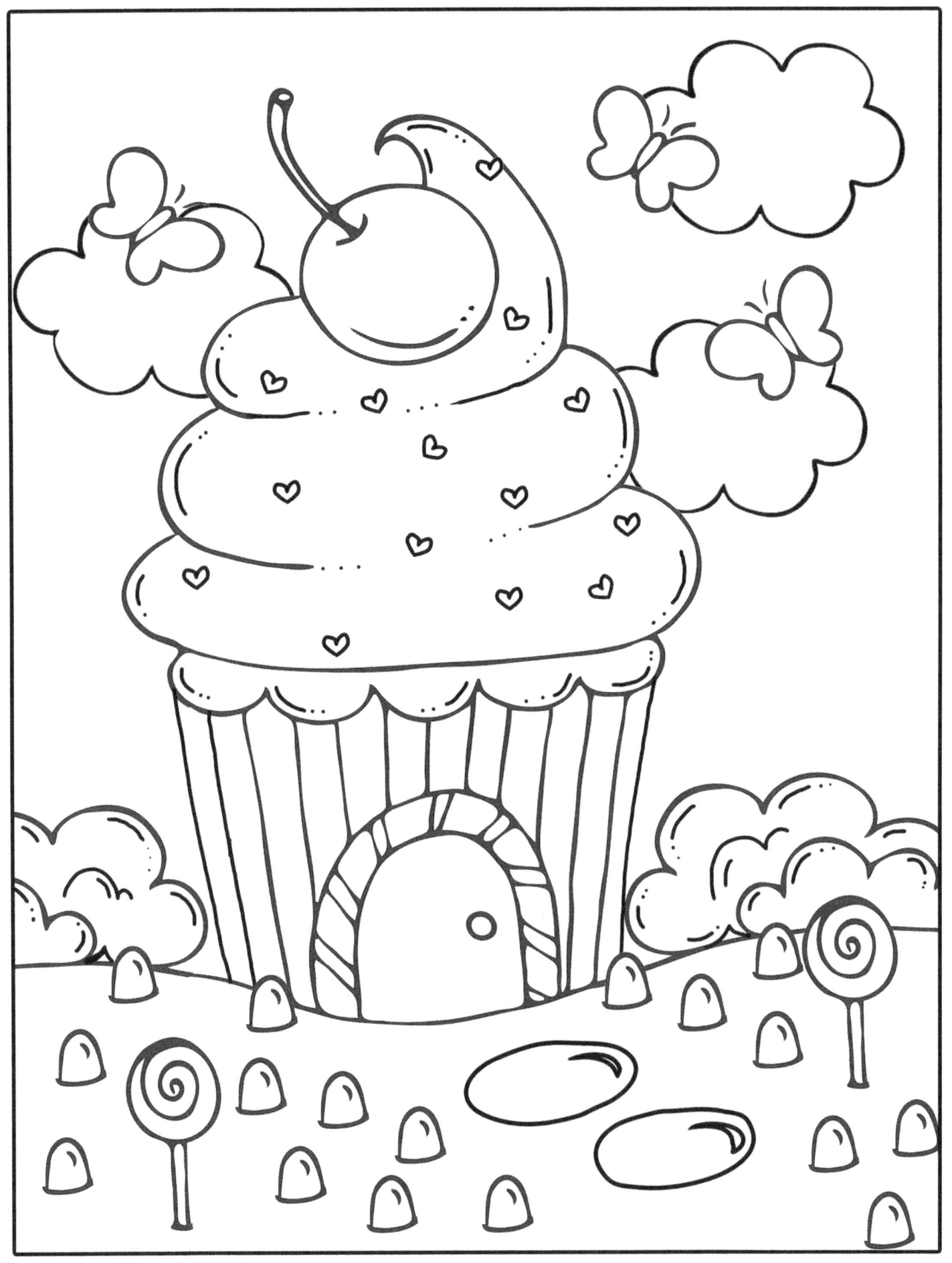

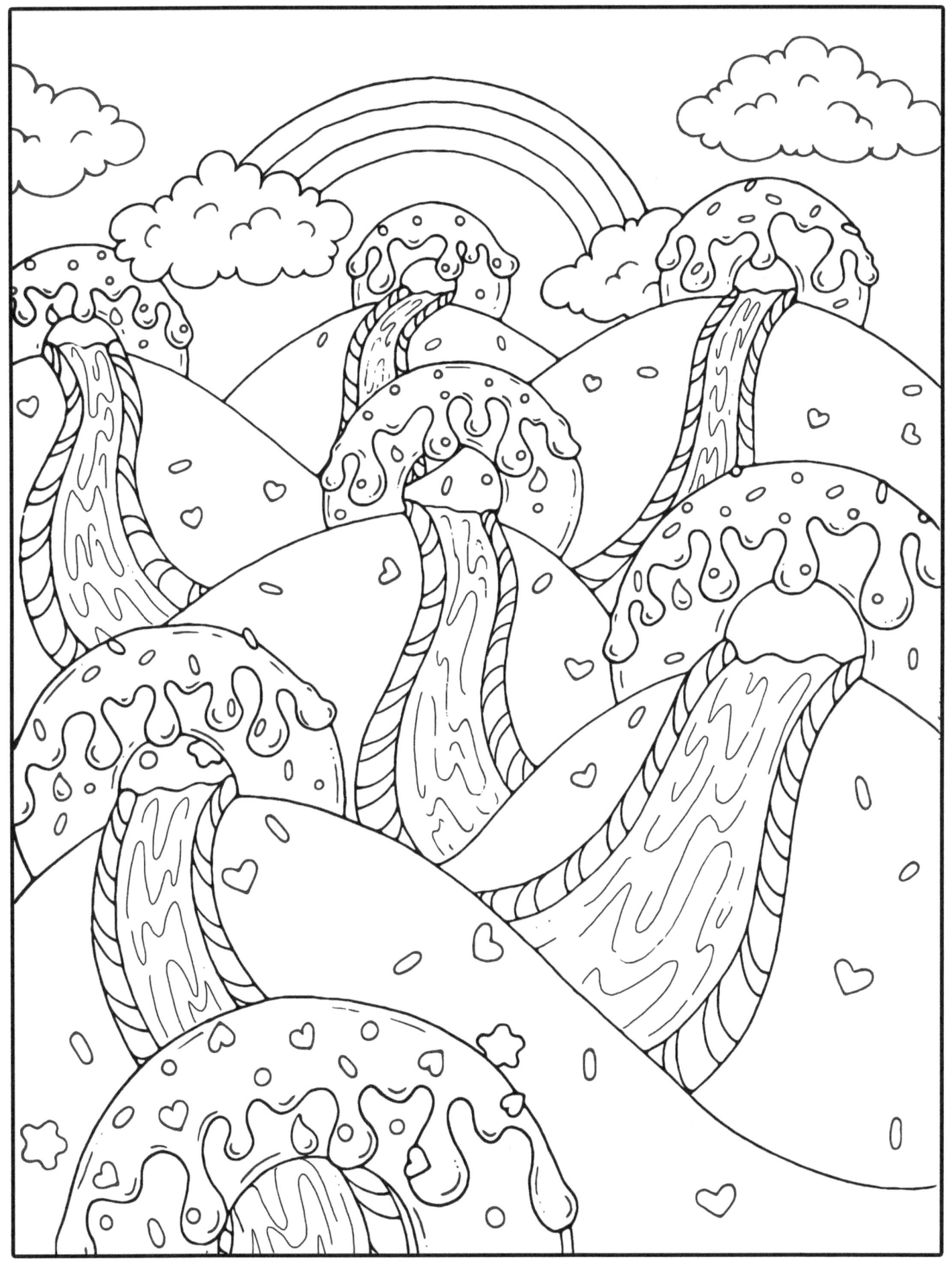

Sweet Retreat ©2019 Tabitha Barnett

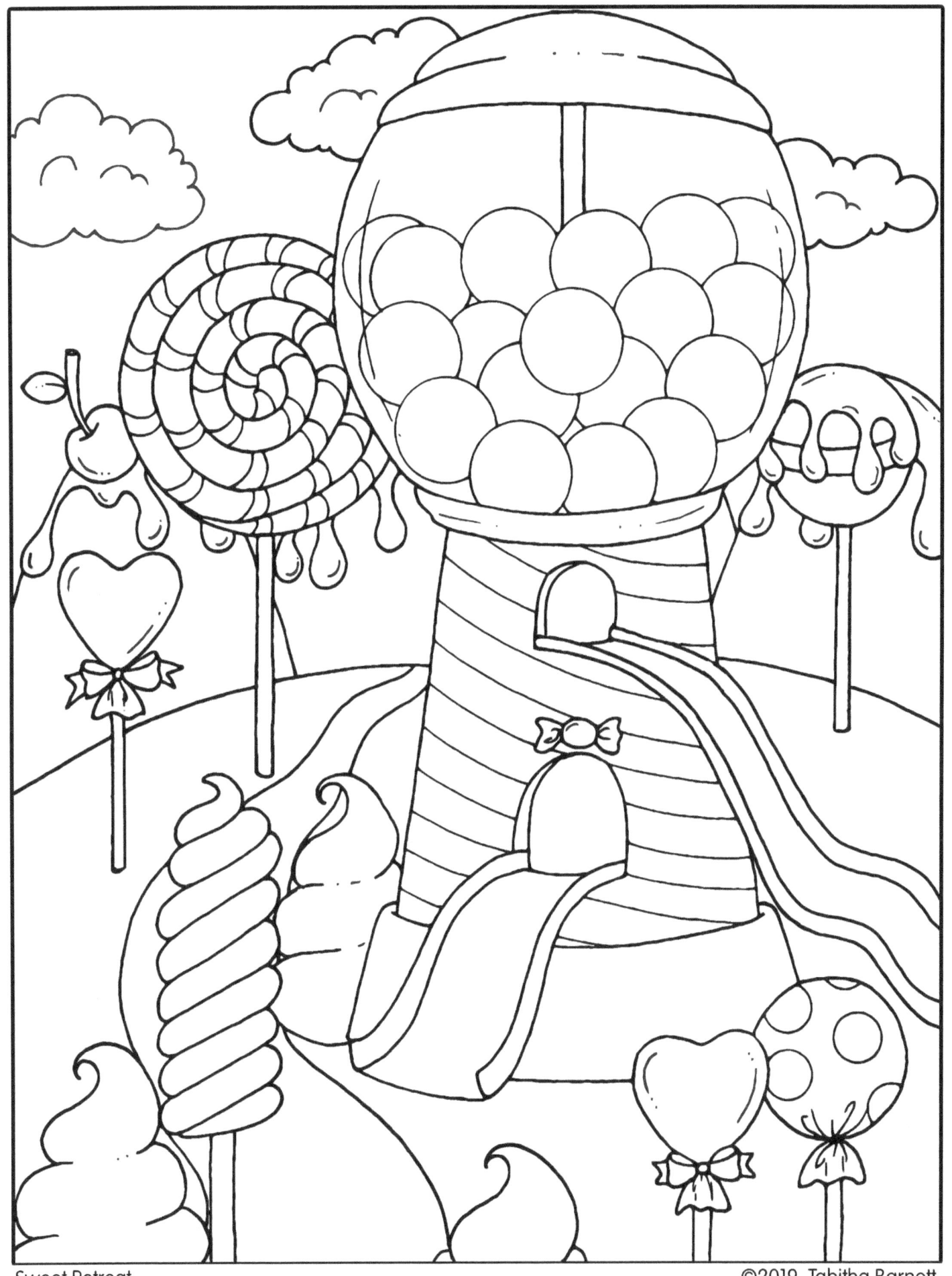

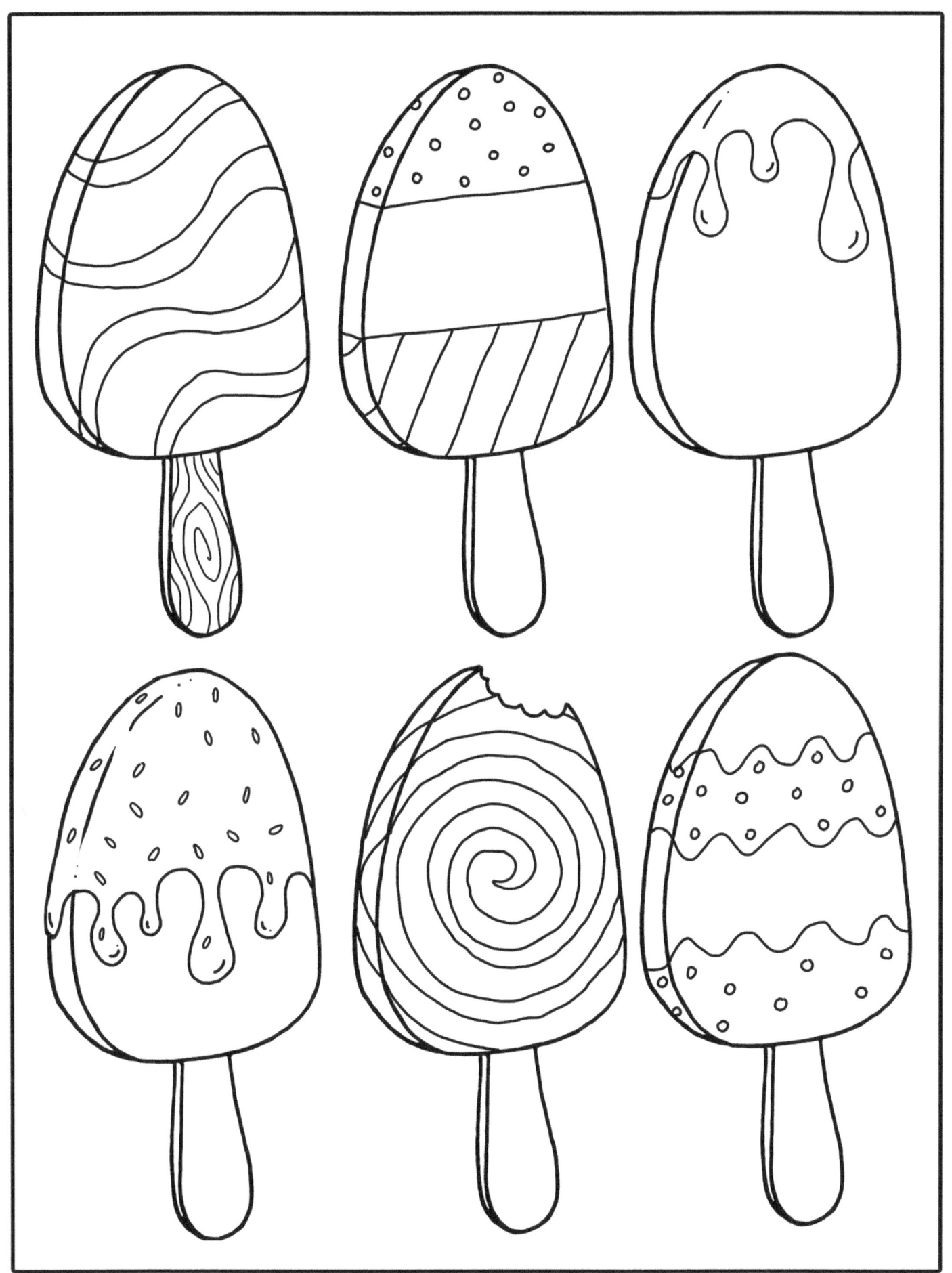

Sweet Retreat ©2019 Tabitha Barnett

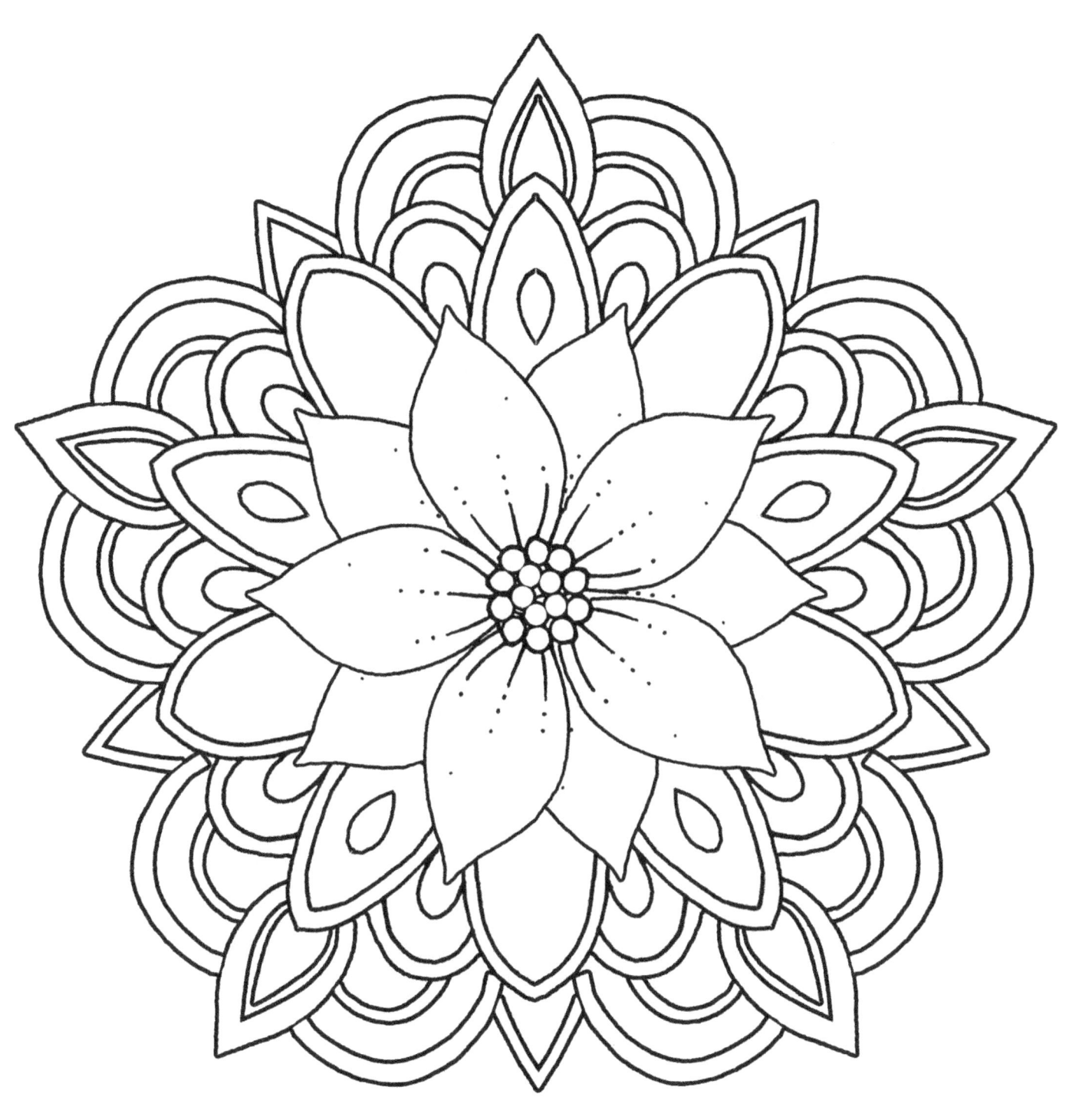

Super Simple Circles ©2019 Tabitha Barnett

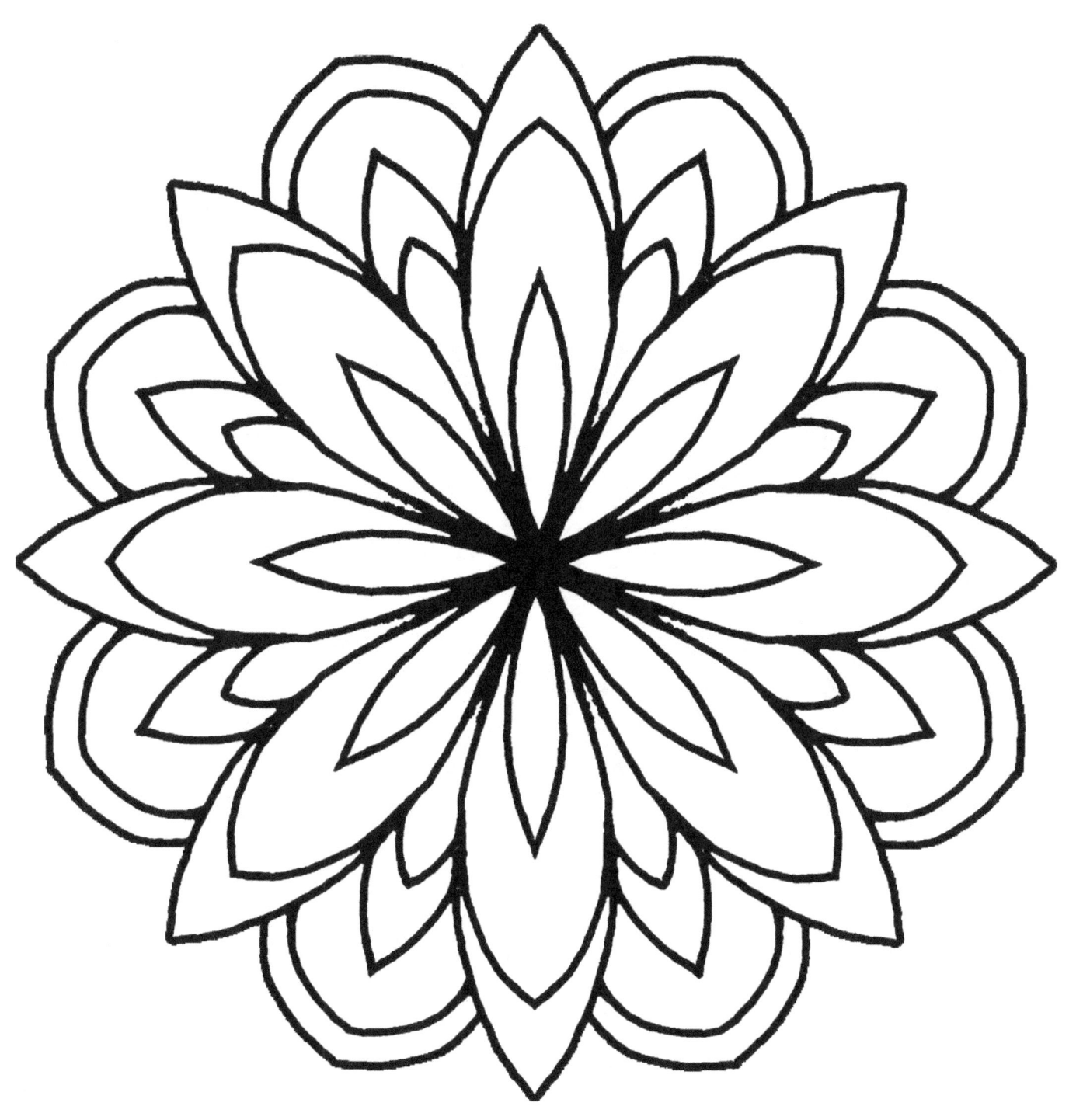

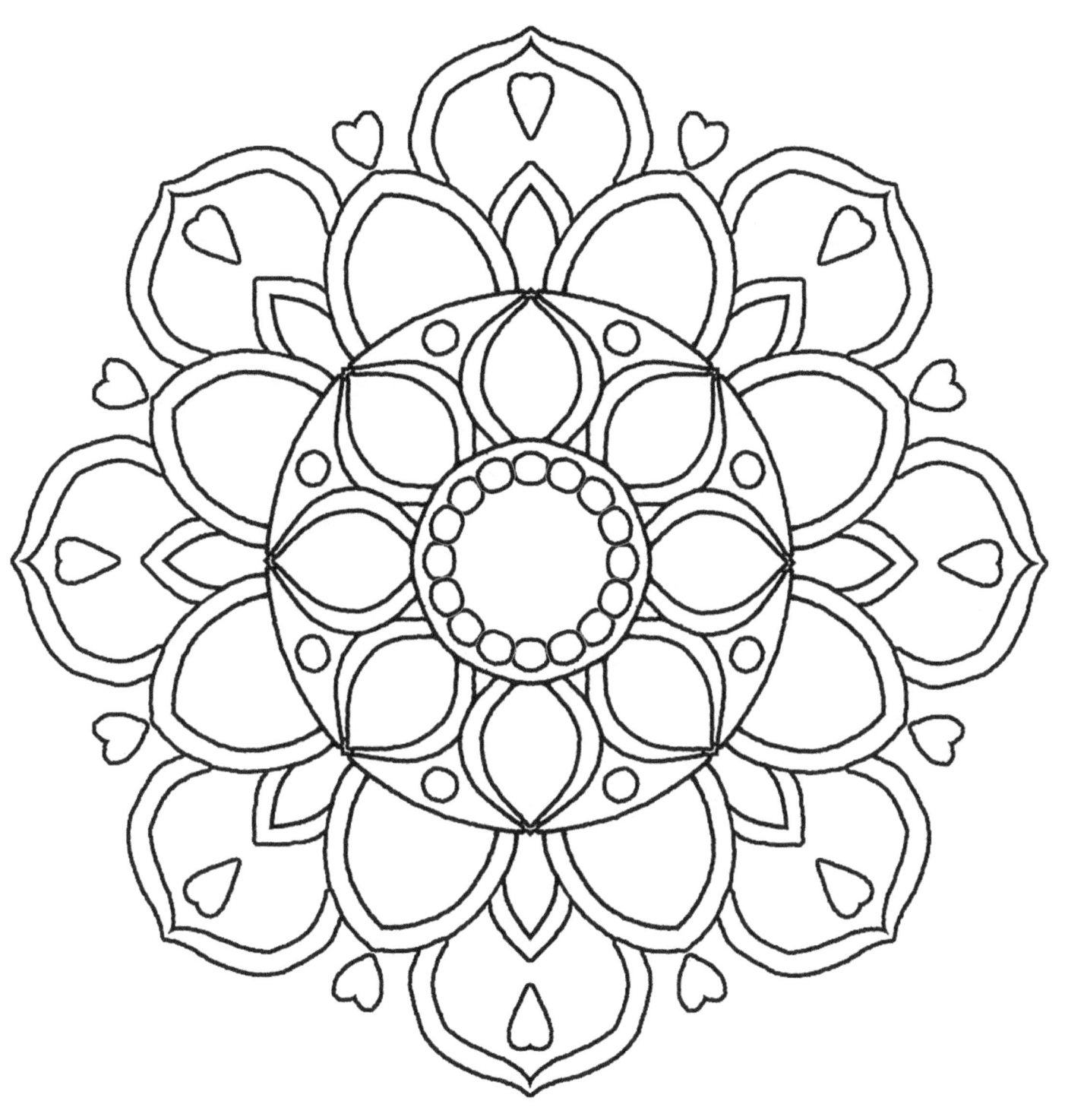

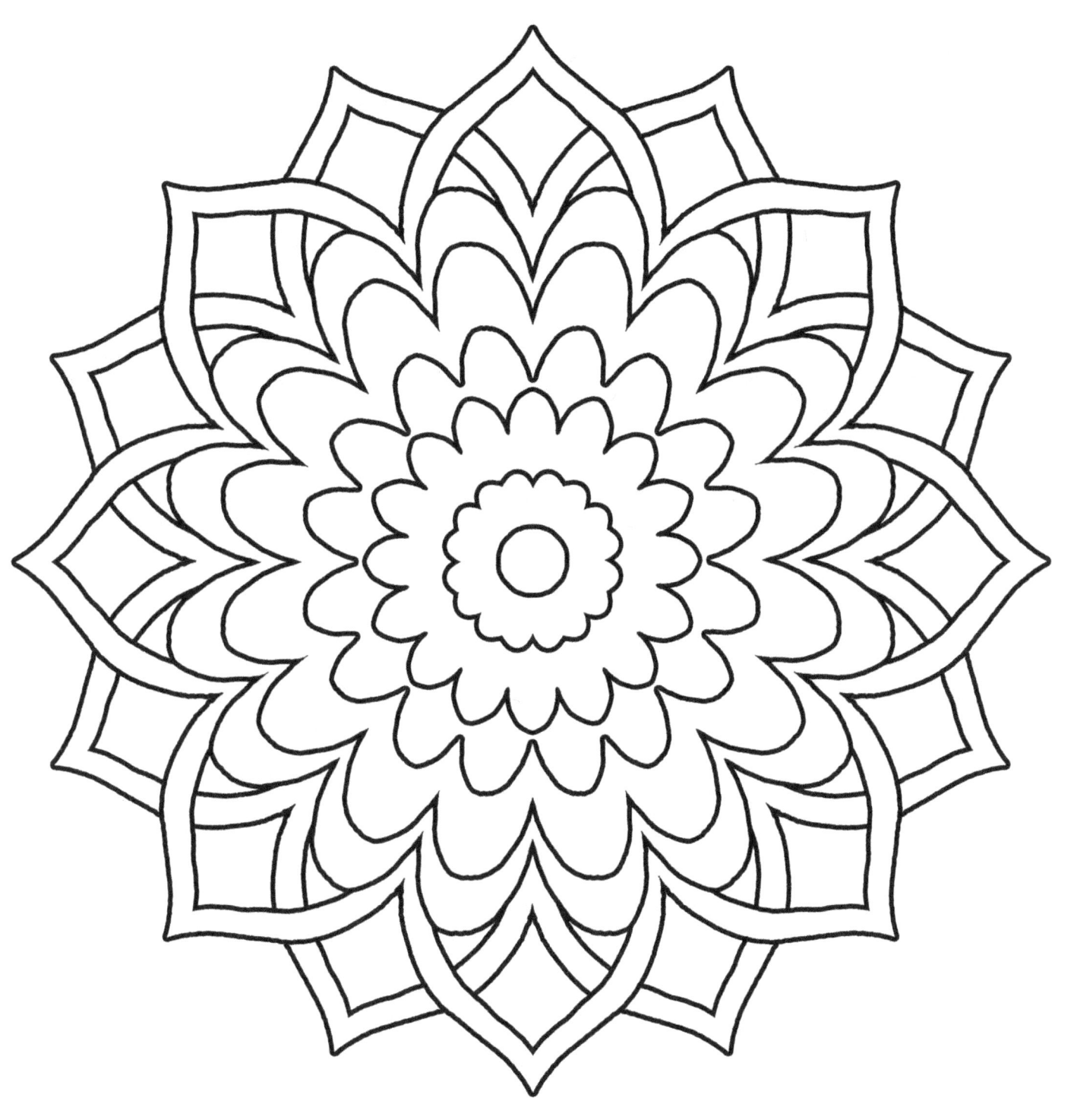

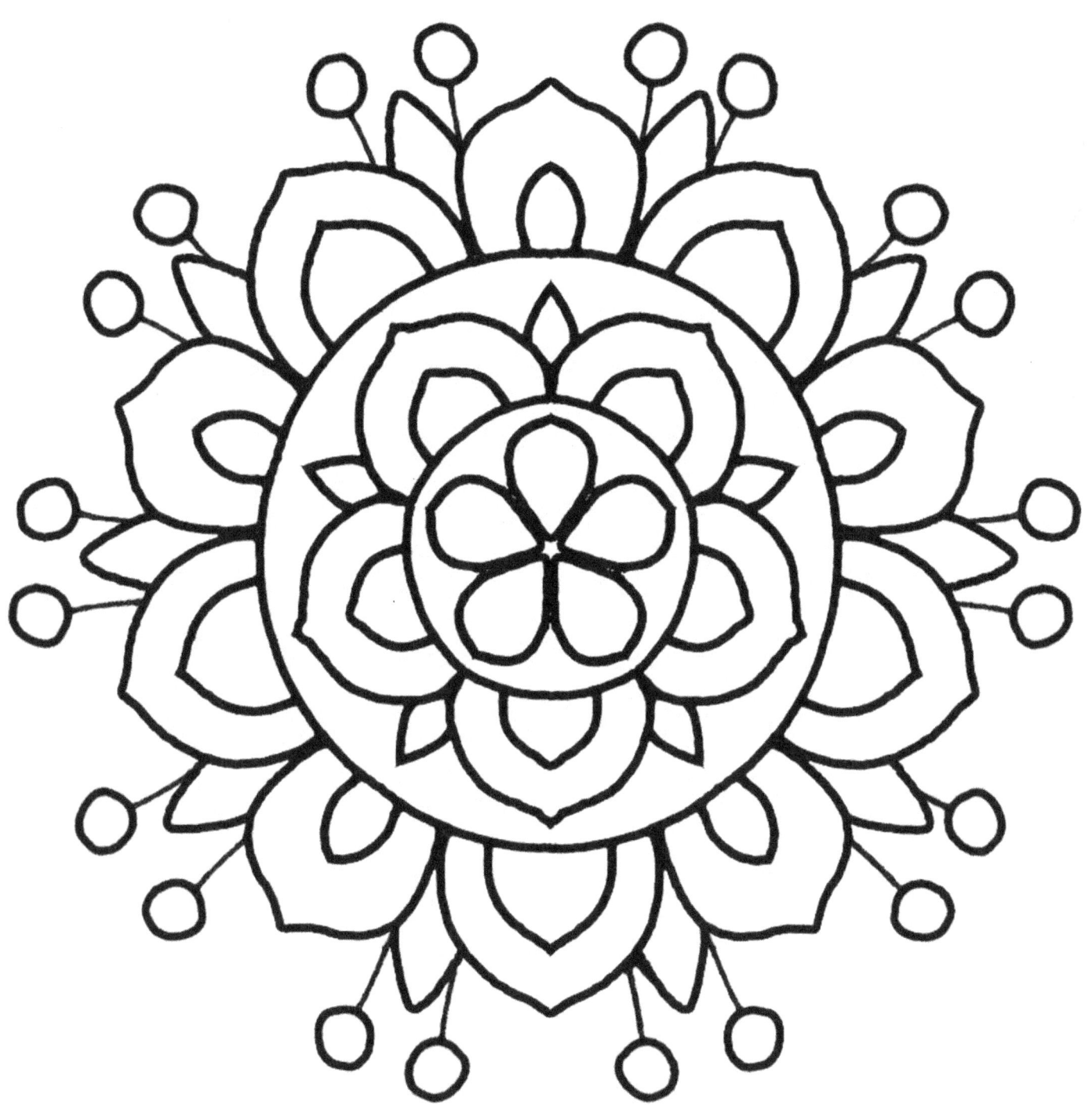

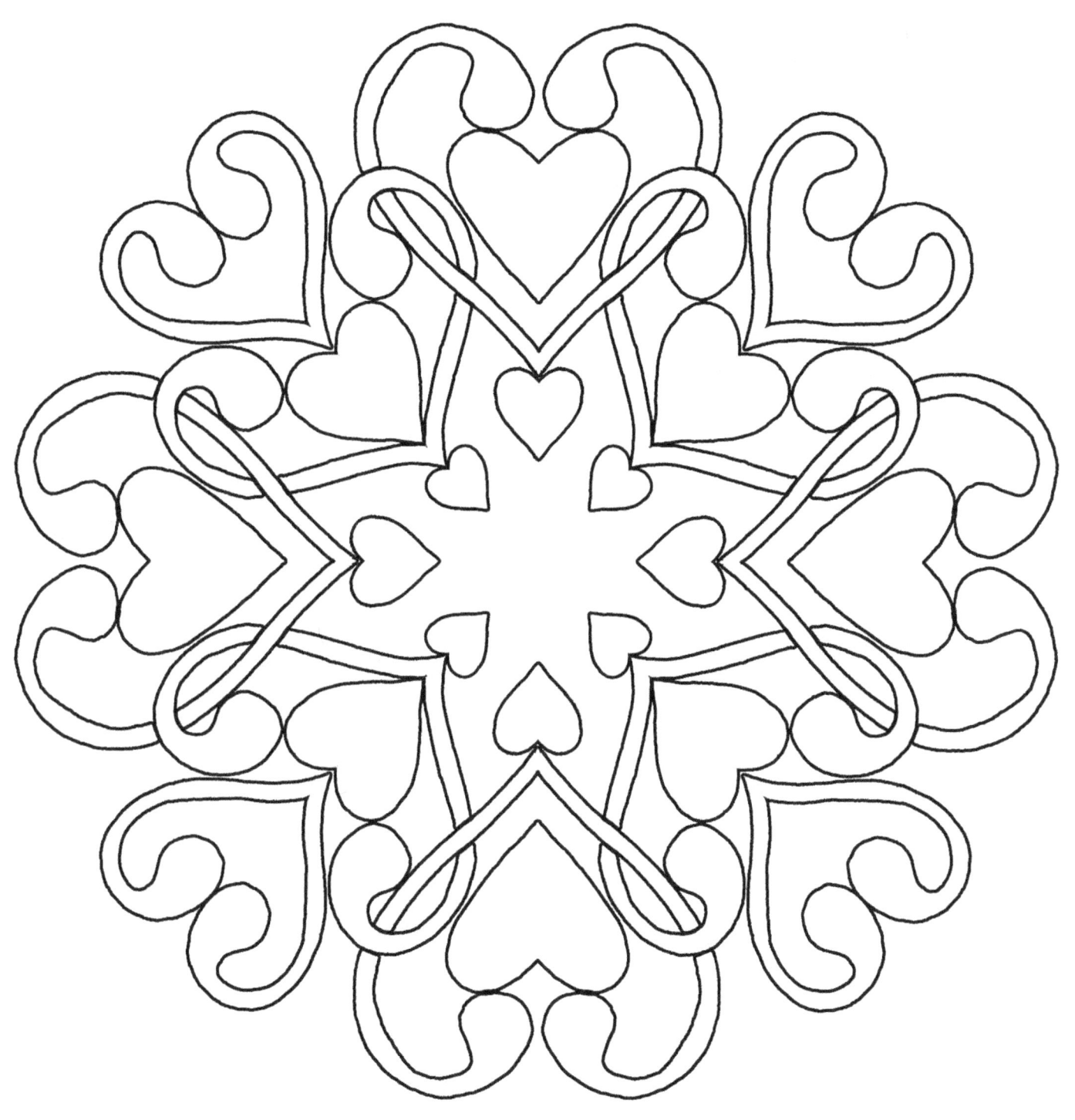

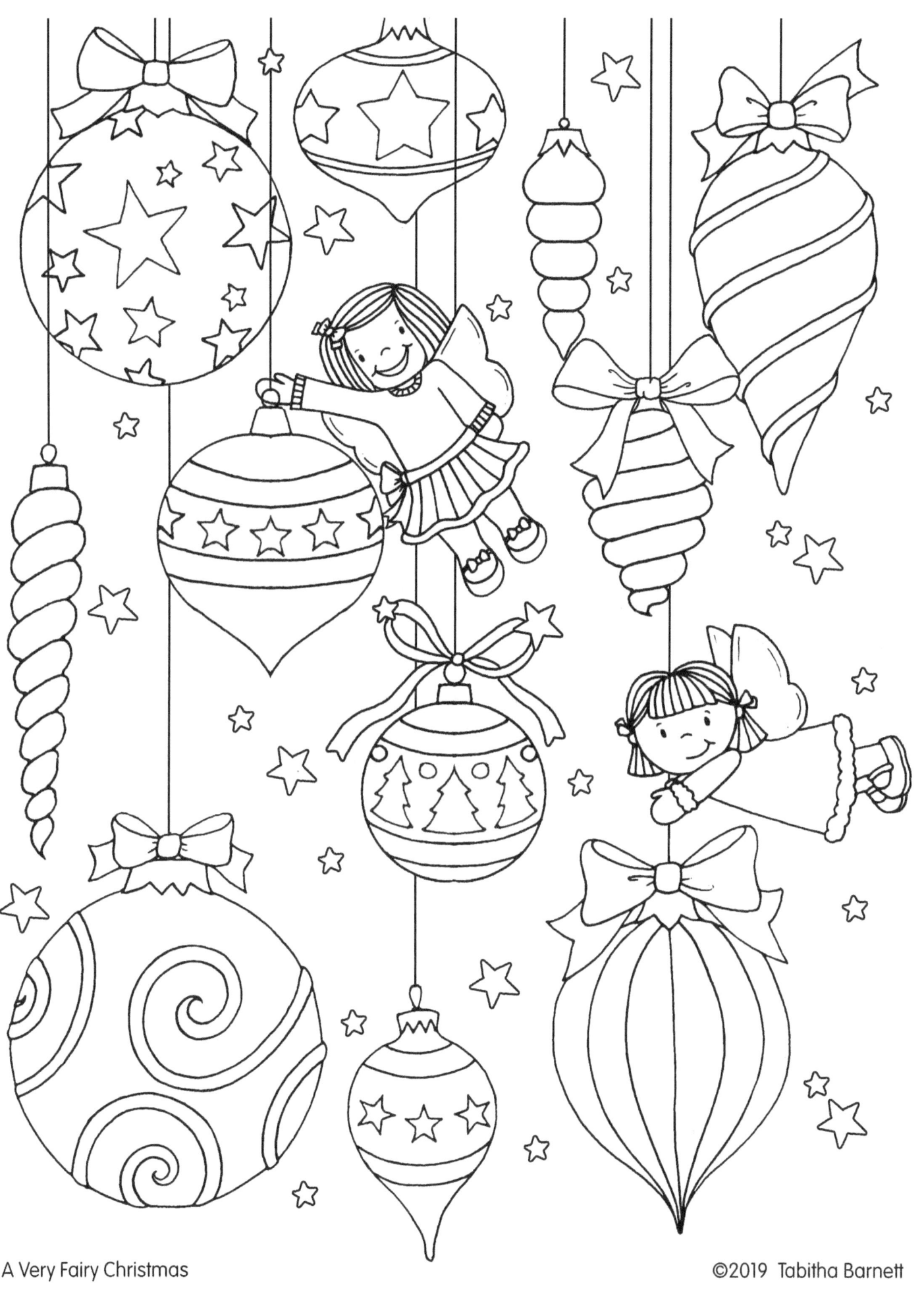

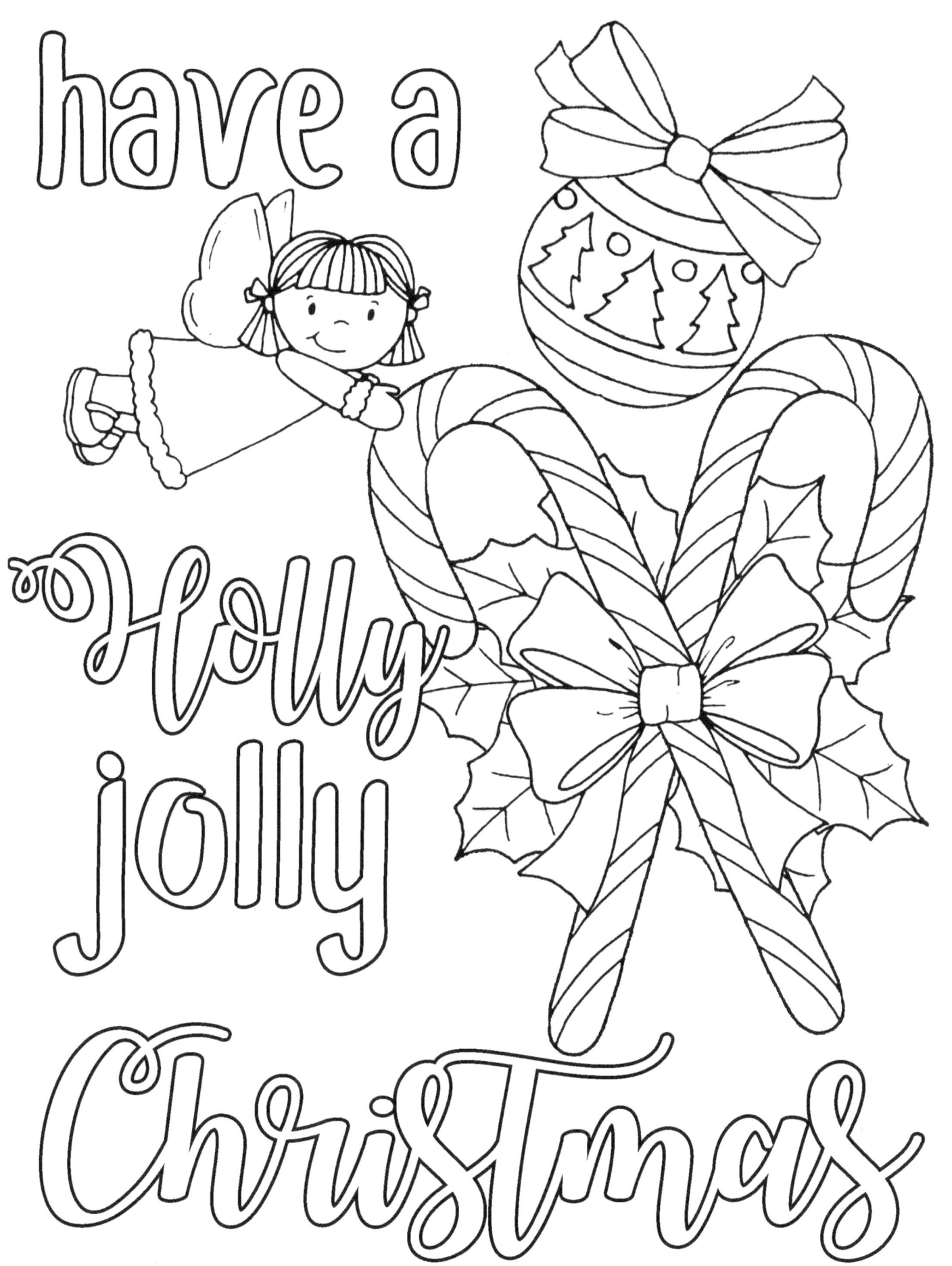

A Very Fairy Christmas ©2019 Tabitha Barnett

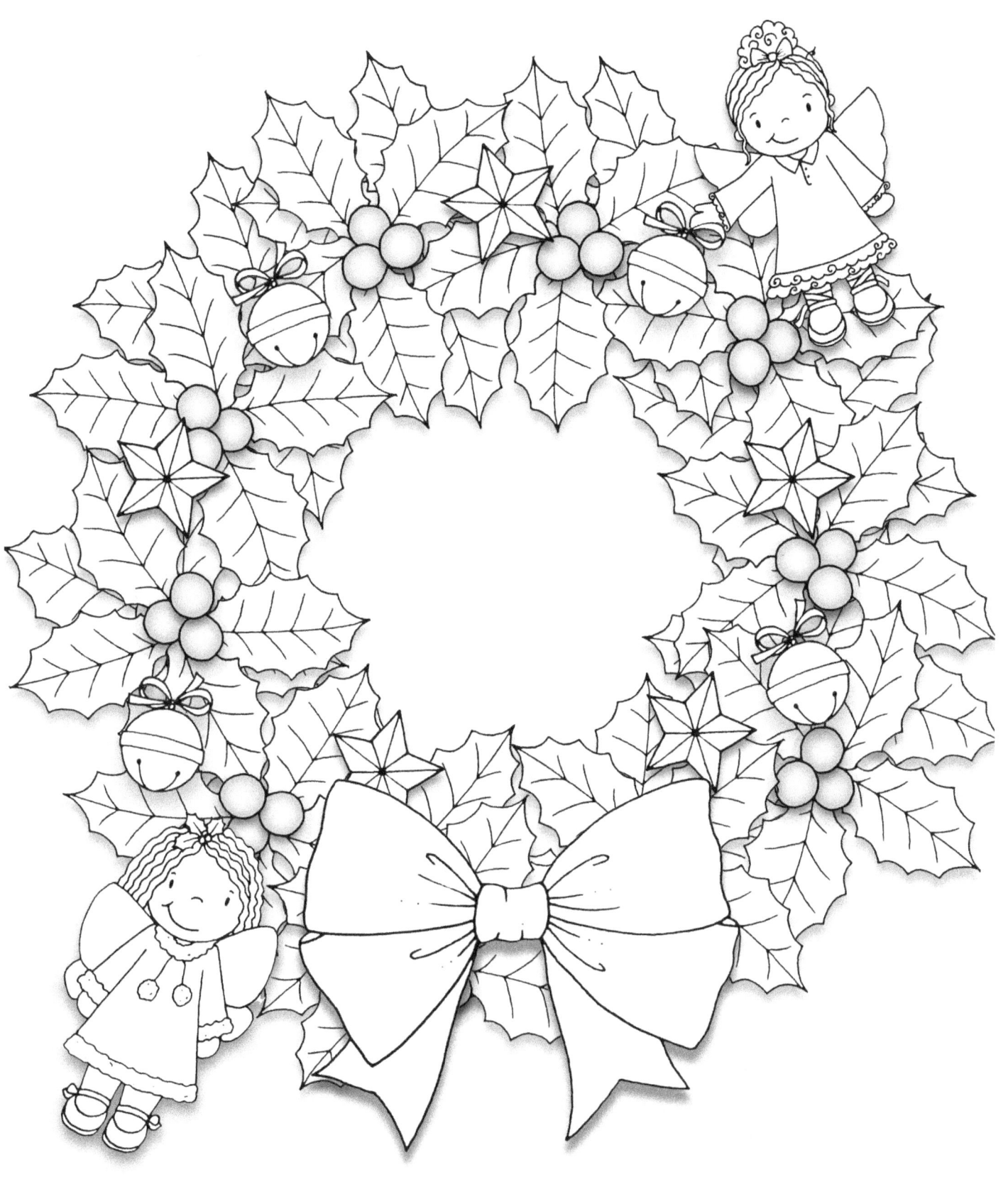

A Very Fairy Christmas ©2019 Tabitha Barnett

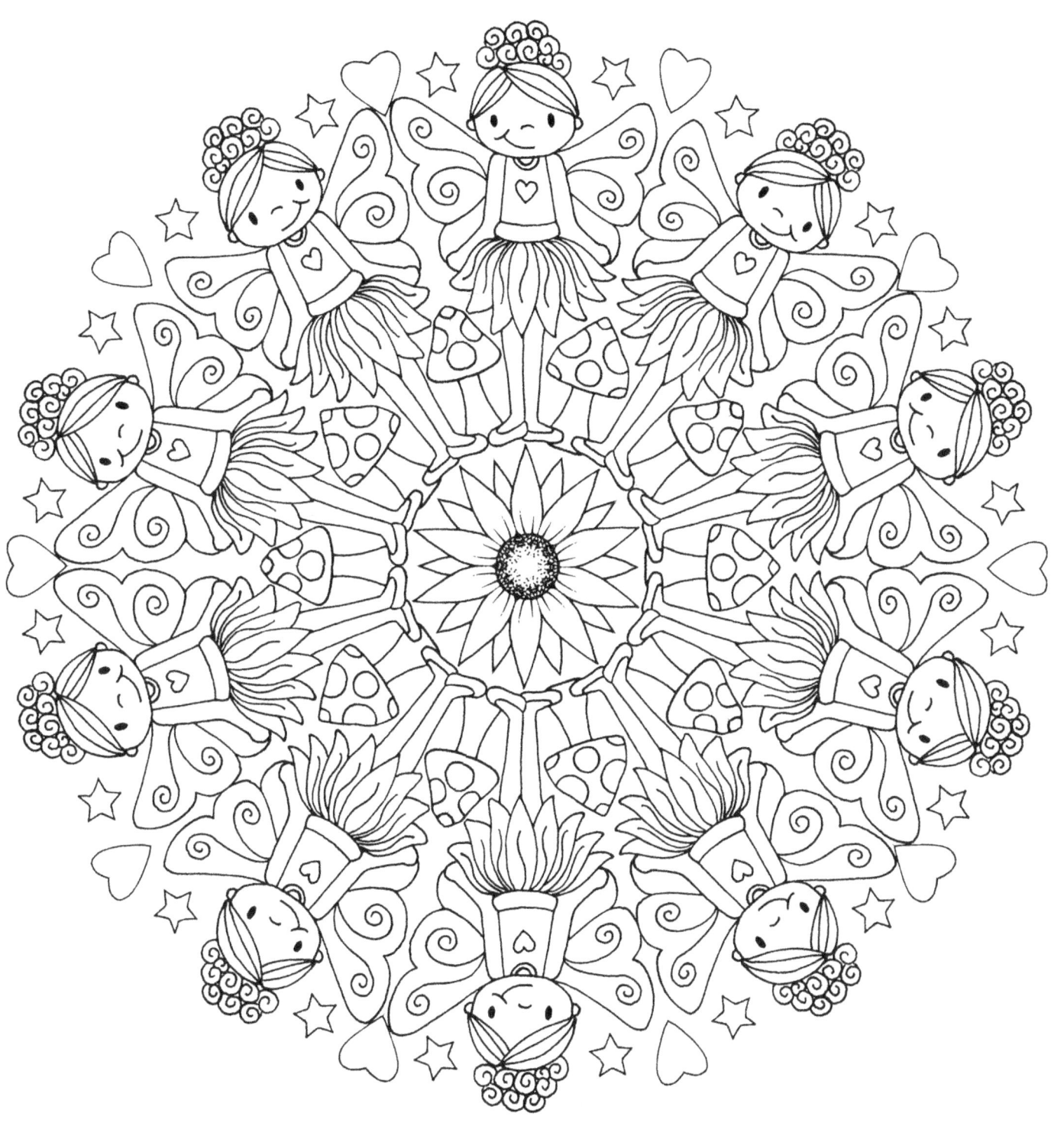

Whimsical Mandalas 1 ©2019 Tabitha Barnett

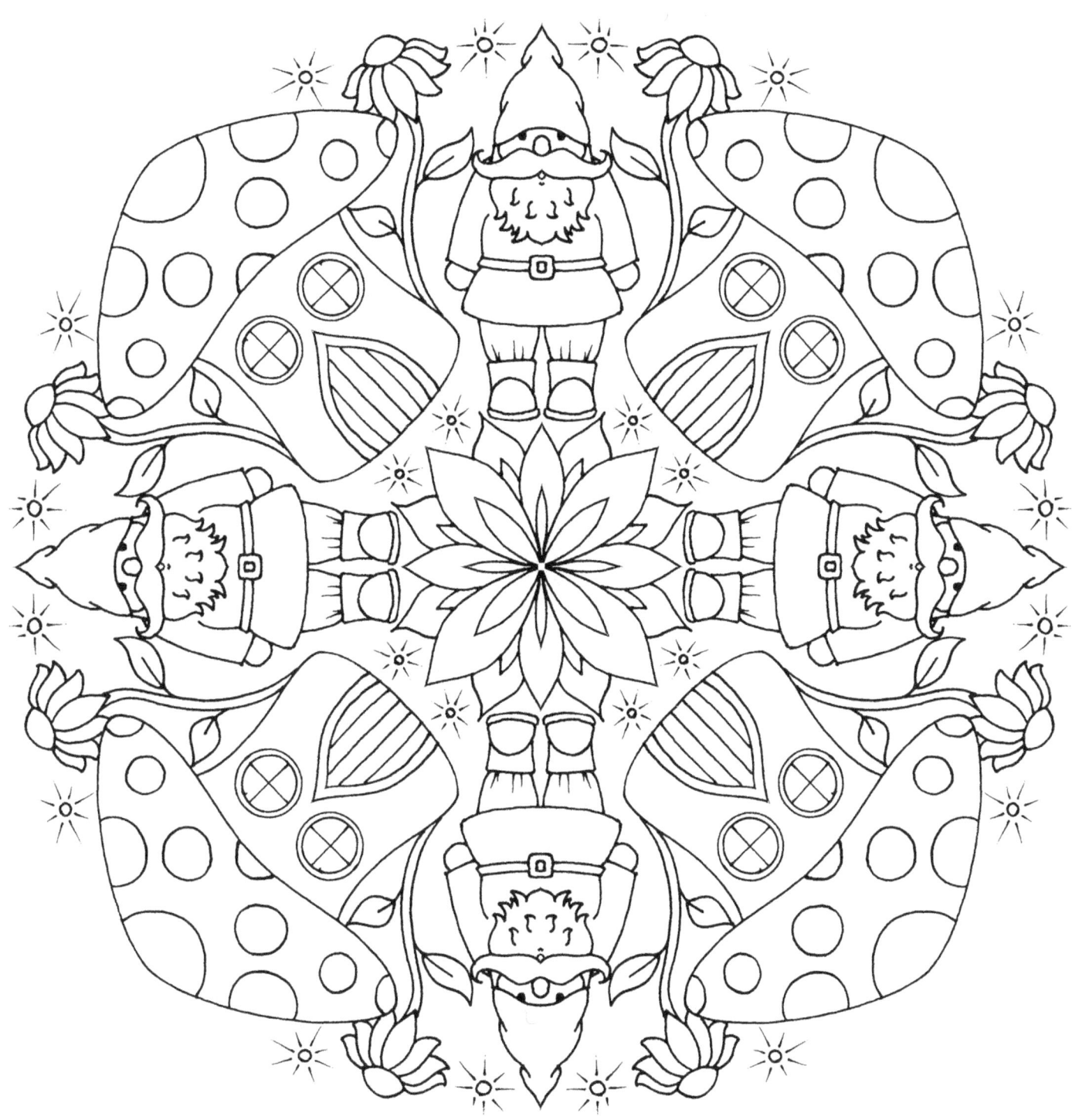

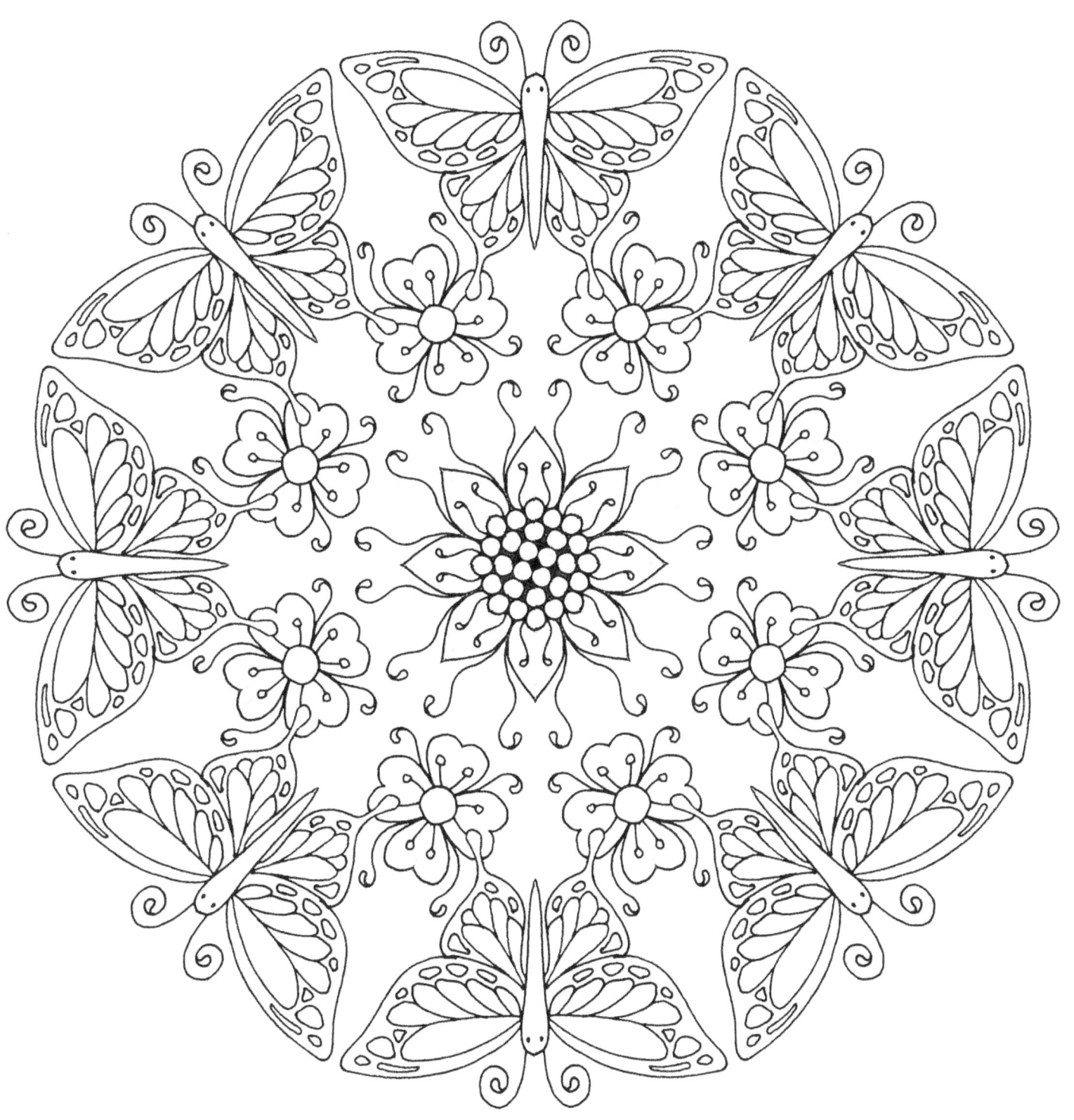

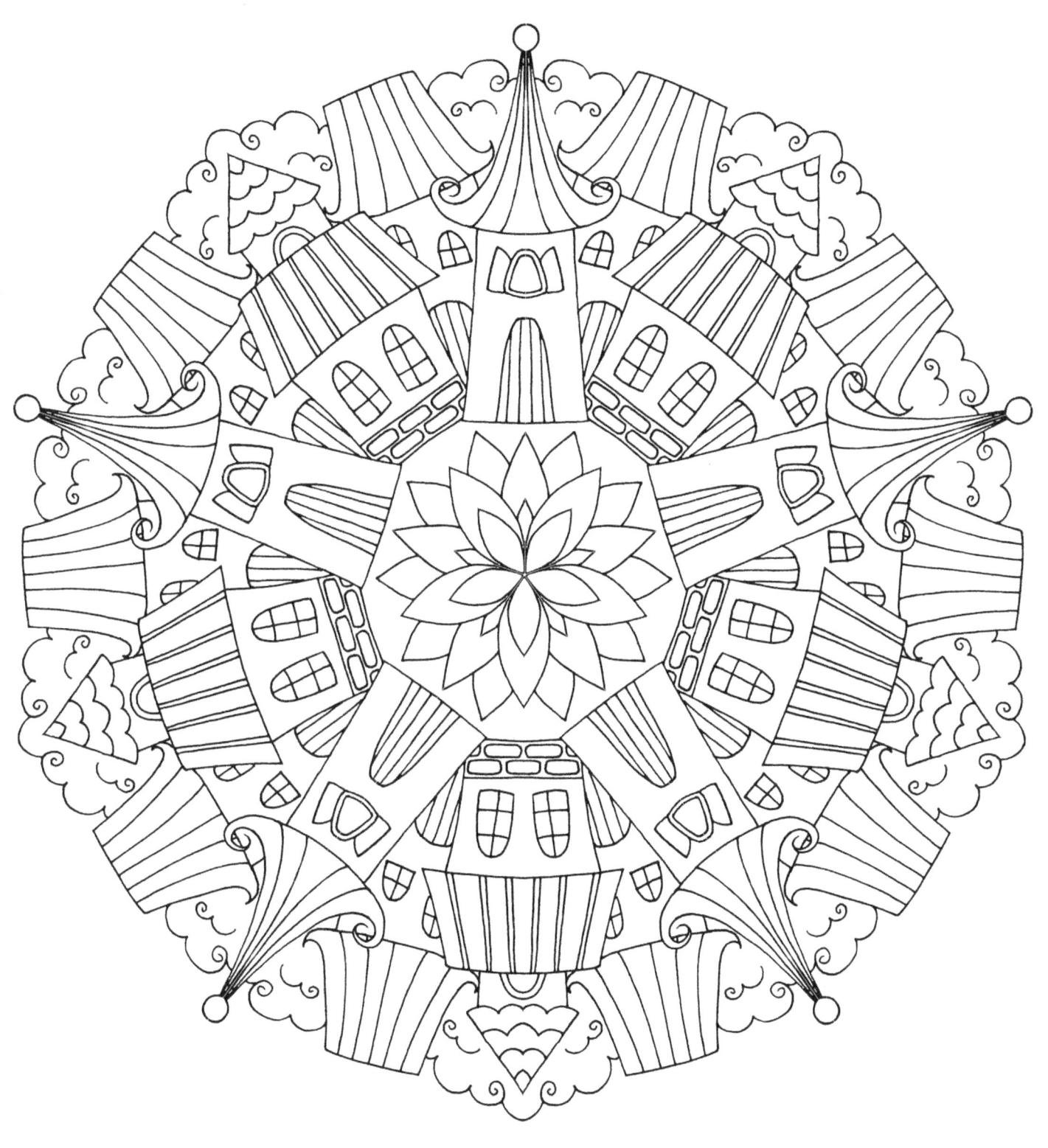

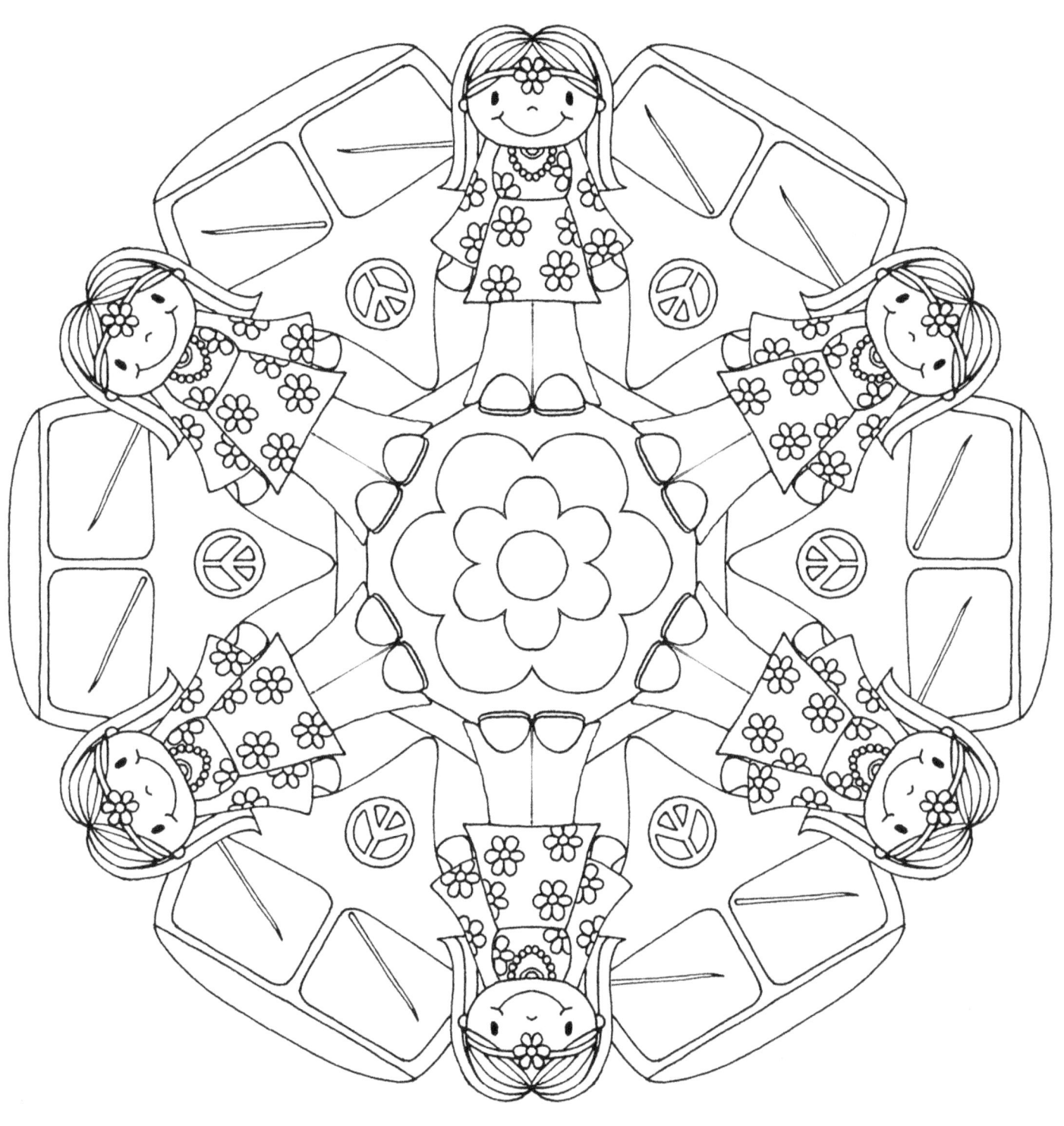

Whimsical Mandalas 2 ©2019 Tabitha Barnett

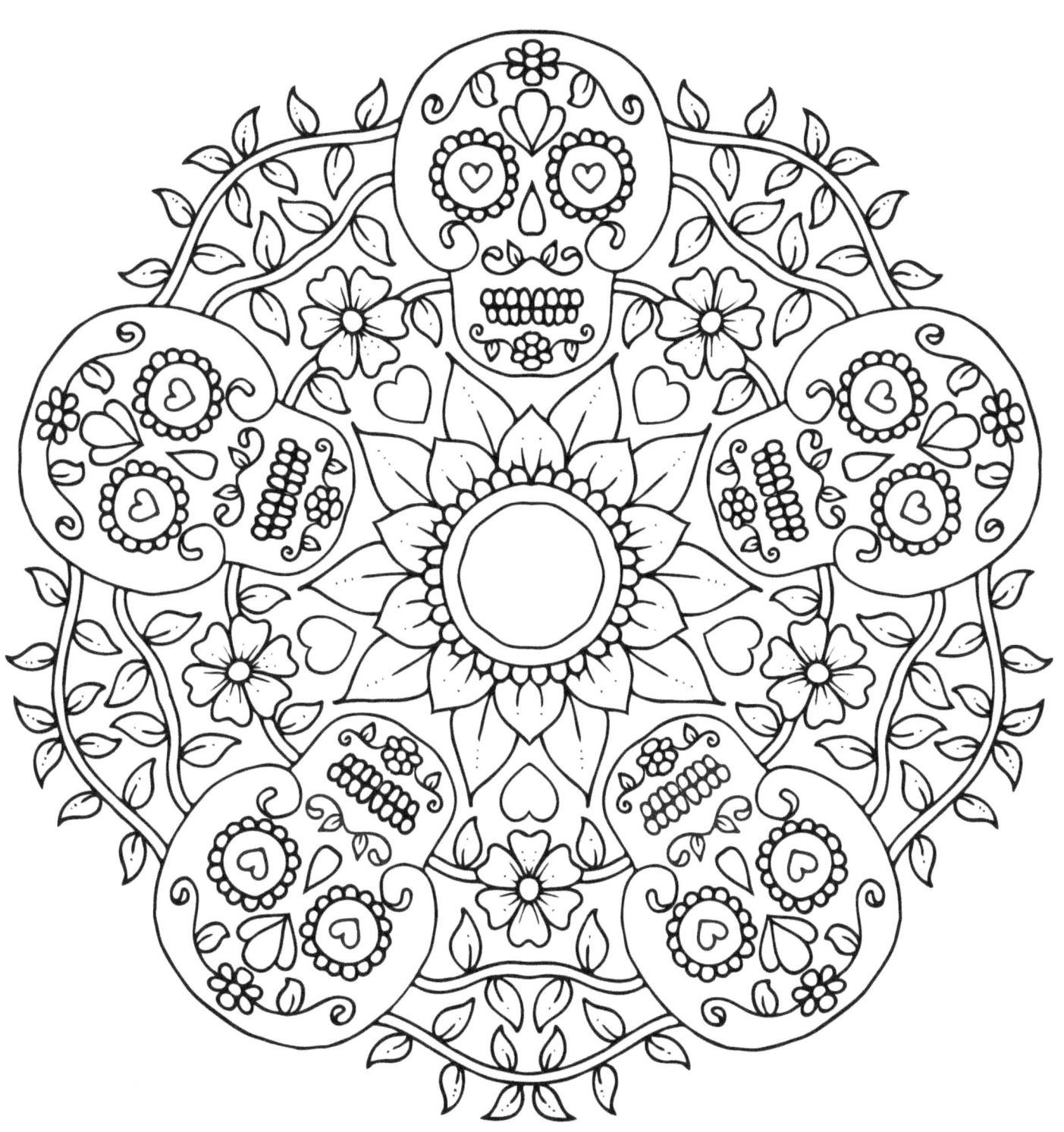

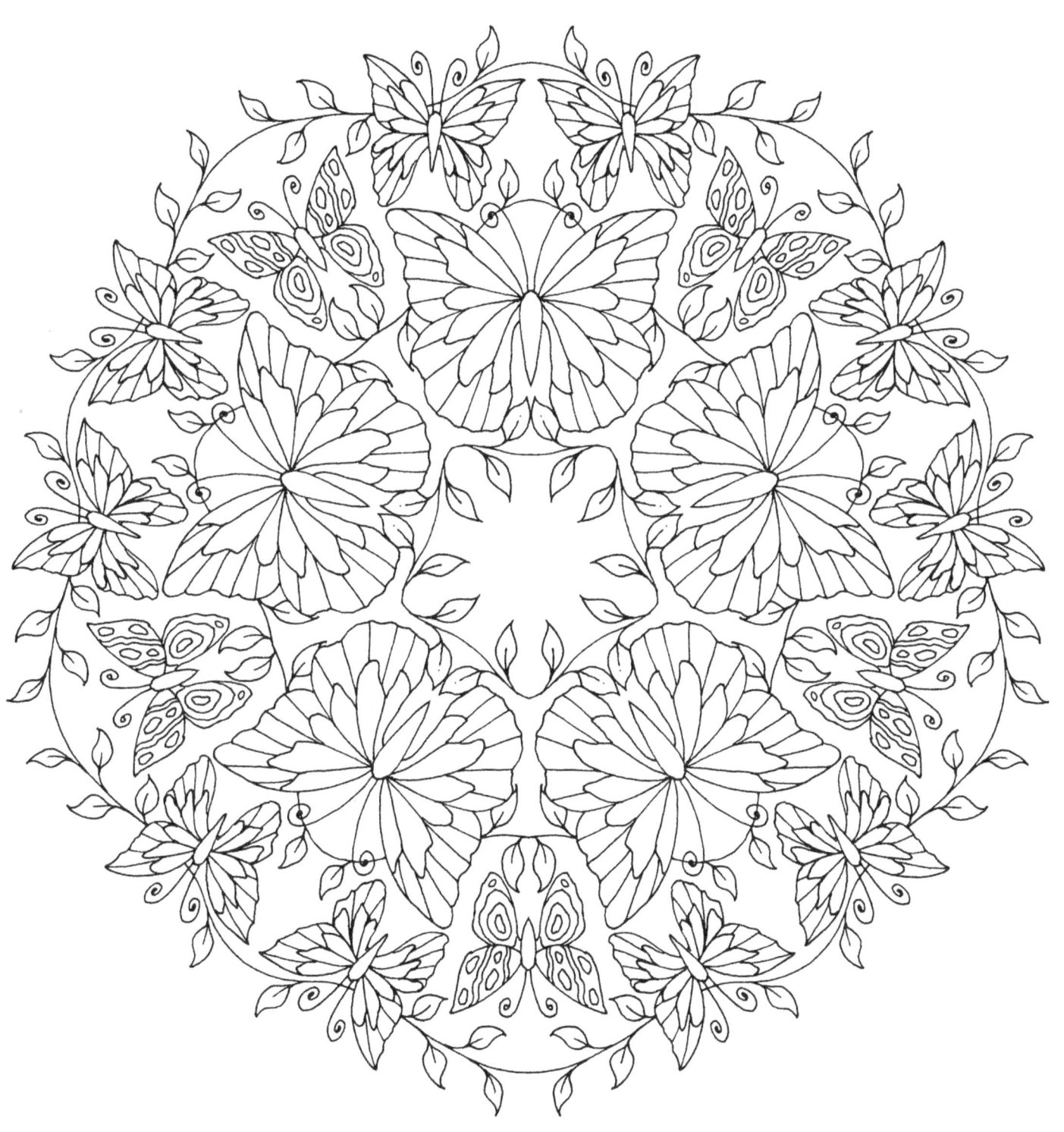

Join the conversation on Facebook:
www.facebook.com/tabbystangledart

If you enjoyed this book, please consider leaving a review on Amazon.

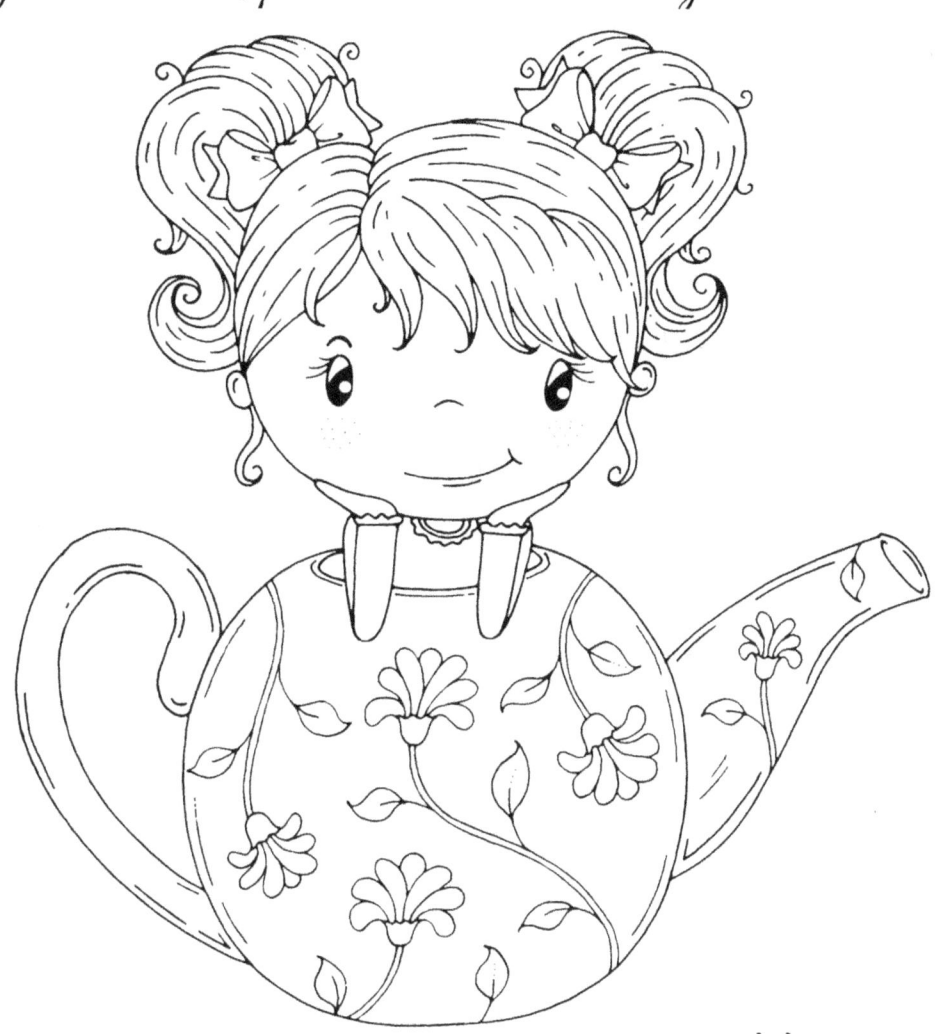

Please post your colored images online using #tabbystangledart or #tabbyb so I can find them easily.

Instagram: @tabbystangledart
Twitter: @tabbyleann
www.patreon.com/tabbyb
www.sellfy.com/tabbyb
www.tabbystangledart.threadless.com
www.redbubble.com/people/tabbyb
www.tinyurl.com/ttavids

COLOR TEST SHEET

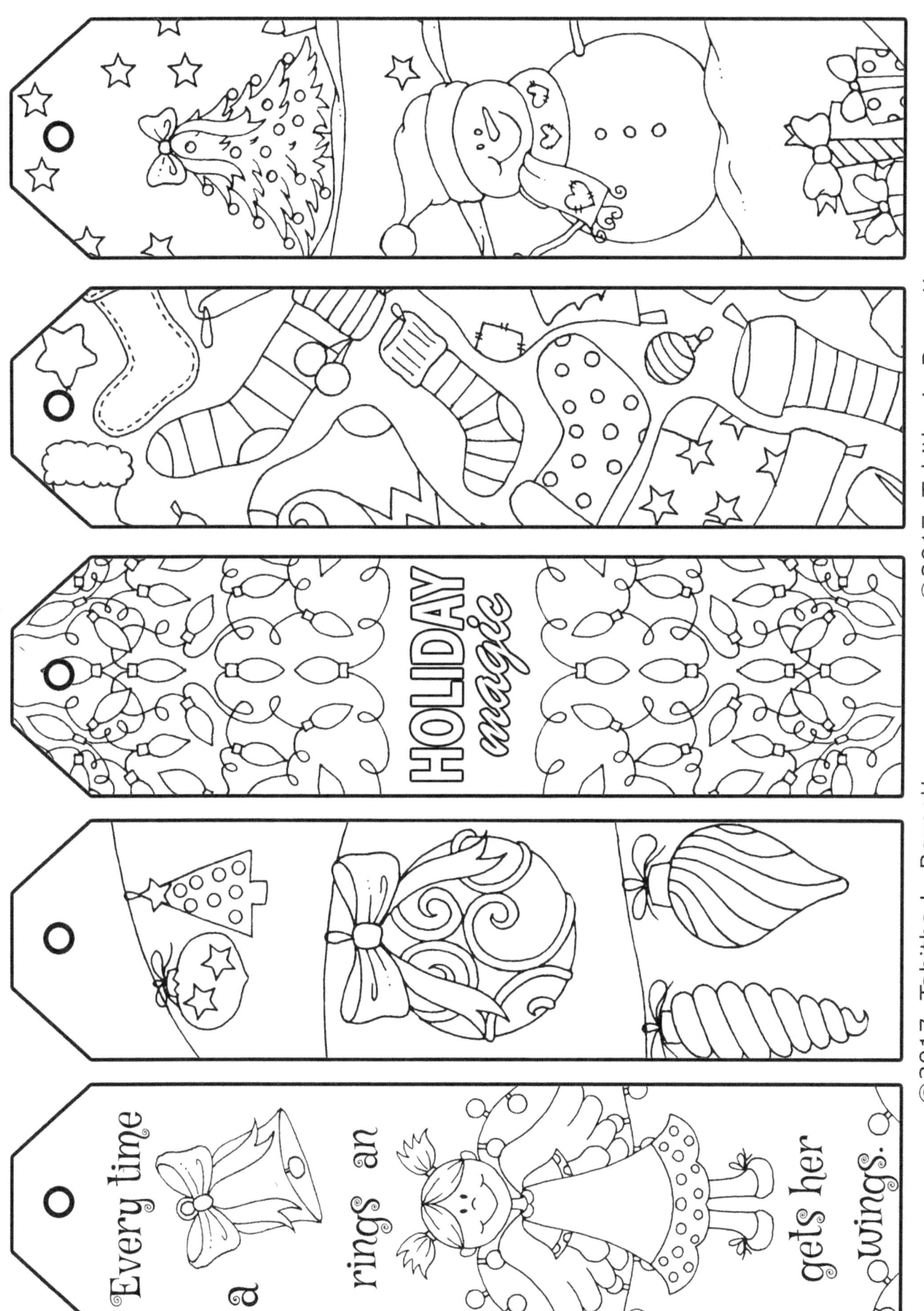

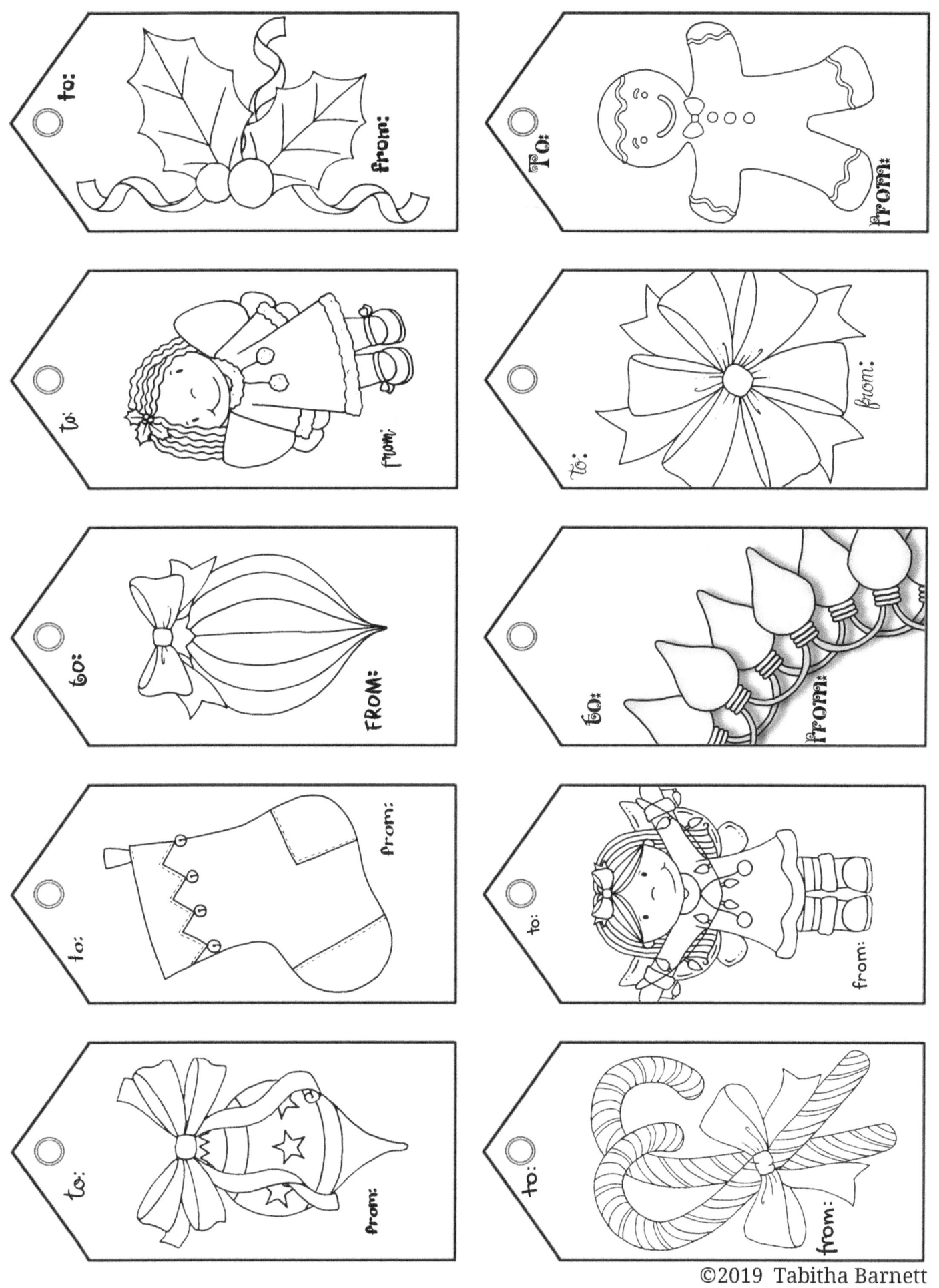

©2019 Tabitha Barnett

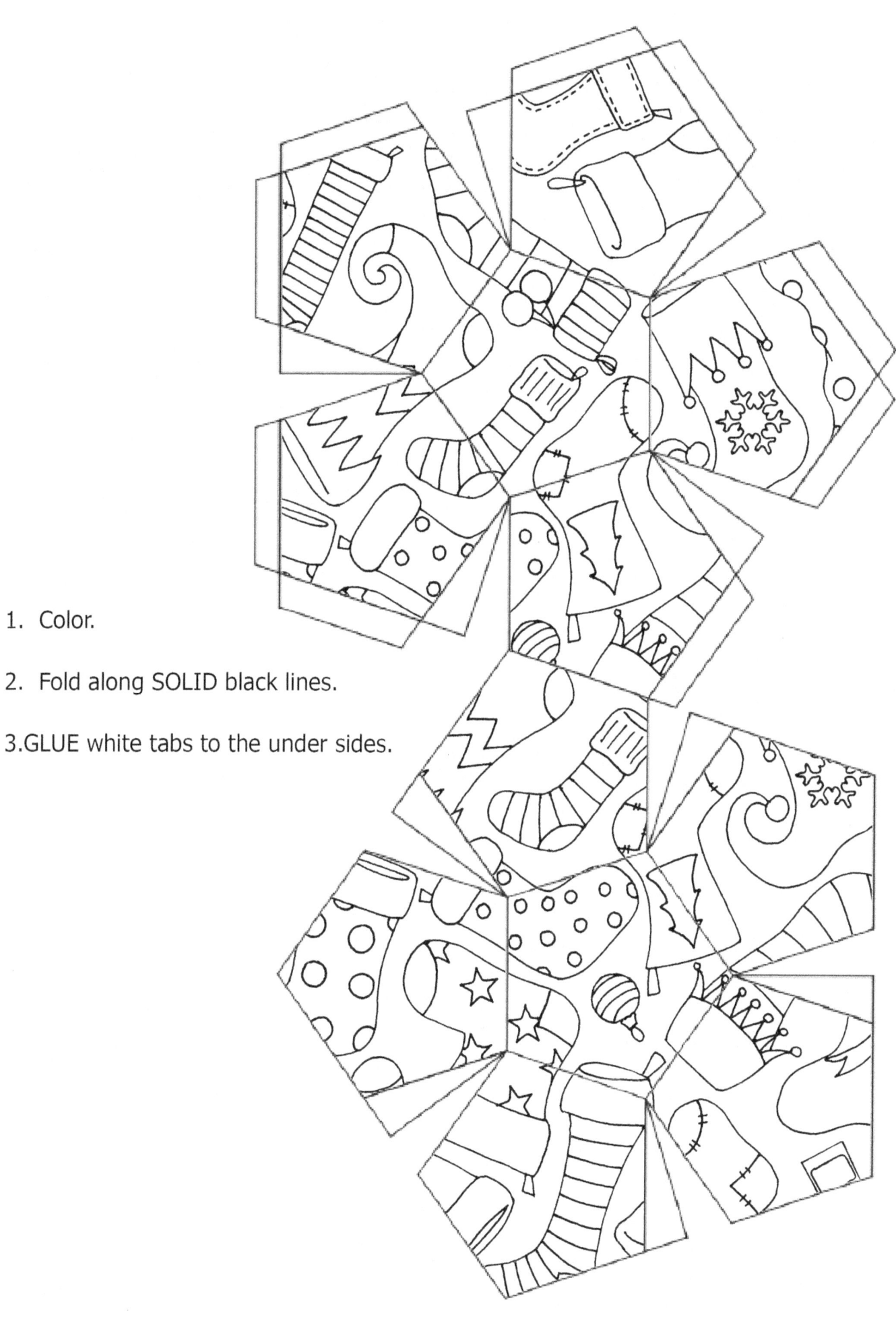

1. Color.

2. Fold along SOLID black lines.

3. GLUE white tabs to the under sides.

www.ingramcontent.com/pod-product-compliance
Lightning Source LLC
Chambersburg PA
CBHW081428220526
45466CB00008B/2306